ROBERT WOOD
JOHNSON

AND HIS

CREDO

A LIVING LEGACY

LILLIAN PRESS

⌘   ⌘   ⌘

Manufactured in the United States

First Edition

Library of Congress Control Number: 2008923338
ISBN: 978-0-615-19594-0

Design and Layout: Karen Kier

LILLIAN PRESS
State College, PA

LillianPressLGF@aol.com

for
Ellen

PREFACE

Robert Wood Johnson was one of the twentieth century's most innovative and colorful business leaders. He built Johnson & Johnson into a world-renowned company and gave new meaning to the need for corporations to serve the public interest. His shrewd intuition and endless flow of ideas often became milestones of progress in his many areas of endeavor.

As early as the 1930s, he proclaimed that business had a moral purpose, indeed a moral imperative, to serve society and the public interest. Most of his fellow industrialists scoffed at this concept, but Johnson responded by writing a corporate "Credo" that would become the best-known and most widely emulated statement of the responsibility that business has to serve the public interest.

Most of all, Johnson was a man of ideas and ideals, which he pursued with the zeal of a crusader. He had a vast range of interests – business, health care, politics, government, the military, mass transportation, architecture, writing, aviation, yachting, and philanthropy – and he relentlessly searched for new and better ways to do things. Always a student of better management techniques, he saw that the nation's hospitals were not being run effectively, so he helped form the first school of hospital management at Northwestern University.

Years before others, he built some of America's most attractive industrial plants, placing them in suburban settings on acres of handsomely landscaped land. It was right after the Depression, and his "Factories Can Be Beautiful" concept set a standard for industry, brought him national recognition, and helped to dispel the impression that industrial architecture had to be ugly. He constructed the nation's first complete textile mill town, with homes, schools, and churches for his workers and their families. He was an innovator who always had a larger purpose. "We build not only structures in which men and women of the future will work, but also the patterns of society in which they will work," he said. "We are building not only frameworks of stone and steel, but frameworks of ideas and ideals."

Two generations before others took up the cry, he was advocating a larger role for women in politics and championing environmental concerns. He had a passion for cleanliness in the workplace – in part because his company made sterile surgical products. He had the corners of manufacturing areas, including the stairwells, painted white so dust and dirt could be easily detected. Once, he shut a plant down for an entire week because of careless housekeeping and told workers and management to get busy cleaning it up. He was a character, and not always a lovable one. But his employees revered and respected him.

He never forgot his early years as a young factory worker, and the old-timers from the mill were the only ones who still called him by his first name. He spoke and wrote about his conviction that the term "common man" was disrespectful. Every individual, he insisted, was entitled to be judged on his or her own merits. "A man's character," he said, "should not be gauged by what he earns." He was once described as being "splendidly Baronial," but few of that ilk ever had a more common touch.

Robert Wood Johnson died in 1968, and for the last ten years of his life I assisted him with various corporate, civic, political, and philanthropic projects. A restless spirit and an incurable idealist, he was an intriguing individual. Still, he was pragmatic in his ways, and his thinking thrust him far ahead of his times.

Johnson's life was like a mosaic, a collection of many and varied parts that, when pieced together, form a larger and more meaningful whole. Close scrutiny reveals imperfections, but the man's flaws add to his humanness. He worked hard at being different from others, and his spirited wit and love of adventure enhance the enjoyment of tracing his footsteps through life.

I will not forget our first meeting. The year was 1957, and I had recently left as night editor of the Newark News, then New Jersey's largest newspaper, to join Johnson & Johnson to help form its first public relations department. The company was still relatively small, with annual sales under $300 million. Shortly before noon that day, a call came from the office of George Smith, the company president, summoning me to meet him promptly in the office of "The General," as he was known. (I later learned that such calls were treated with the same degree of concern as fire alarms.) Unfortunately, however, I was not in the office, having taken an early lunch hour to rummage through a local auto junkyard in search of a part for my aging car.

When I returned to the office quite a while later, I was told to report immediately to the General's office. I arrived there about the same time as a very agitated George Smith, and for the first time took the long walk from the entrance to Johnson's office to his circular desk in the corner of the room. Smith introduced me with a brand of gallows humor I had last heard from a very annoyed city editor.

"General, this is Larry Foster. When he was with the newspaper, he took a half-hour for lunch. Now it seems he takes an hour and a half."

Johnson rose, shook my hand, and without a hint of a smile, said, "Well, young man, I'm glad to see that you are growing in your job."

I knew right then that I would like him.

As I came to know this remarkable person – the range of his accomplishments and the adventures that made up his life – the idea of writing this biography was born. The prospects of writing the book helped feed the journalistic fire that still burned within me. Quietly, I started what ultimately became a vast amount of research on his life's work. In later years, after he died, I interviewed scores of people who knew him, including many members of his family. Along the way, I concluded that in order to maintain independent thought, the book about his life would have to wait until I retired from the company so that my objectivity would not be compromised.

Over the years several authors had approached Johnson about writing his life story, but he always brushed them aside, saying, "I'm not old enough yet." Late in 1967 I wrote him in Florida and asked if we could sit down and, in the interest of recording the company's history, talk about his recollections. That appealed to him. He wrote back that at present he wasn't feeling well and planned to enter a New York hospital for treatment, but that later we would get together. He died in the hospital, and I was asked to write the eulogy delivered at his funeral. Later I wrote a company-sponsored book on the history of Johnson & Johnson, titled A Company That Cares.

After a sometimes errant youth, Johnson settled down. Within fifteen years he worked his way up to become company president, and under his leadership Johnson & Johnson experienced phenomenal growth. Spurred by the success of Johnson's baby products – which became synonymous with motherhood – Johnson & Johnson became one of the world's most admired companies. Under his leadership, the company grew dramatically – from $11 million to $700 million in sales. But it wasn't sales and marketing success that brought Johnson wide acclaim as one of the twentieth century's most visionary business leaders.

He enjoyed his wealth and the pleasures it brought him. But the creation of wealth, he felt, must have a greater goal than merely acquiring money. Long after his death, his sense of personal responsibility toward society is expressed imperishably in the disposition of his immense fortune – more than $1 billion – which he left to The Robert Wood Johnson Foundation to improve health and healthcare in America.

He loved a good battle, and engaged in many, including one memorable period in Washington during World War II when President Franklin D. Roosevelt appointed him to a high government post. He served as a one-star general for all of sixty days before losing out in a confrontation with the Pentagon brass. On his retreat from the capital, he snidely remarked to columnist Walter Winchell that Washington was "a magnet for mediocrity," one of the scores of quotable comments that endeared him to journalists. Wry humor was his constant companion. His politics swung wildly from conservative to liberal, depending on the issue, and made him unpredictable. He was the only one in the history of New Jersey's turbulent politics to be offered the nomination for U.S. Senate by both the Republican and Democratic parties in the same election year.

Fiercely patriotic, he had a profound sense of duty and spoke openly of love of country. Once, when he felt that democracy was being threatened by communism, he declared: "It is our responsibility to do something every day of our lives, however inconsequential, to support the American Constitutional principles." His allegiance to his country glowed in his widely acclaimed book Or Forfeit Freedom. He left his mark in other ways too. In mid-century, when employee relations in the nation were at a low ebb, he rallied a group of national leaders and took the lead in writing a document titled "Human Relations in Modern Business," an action plan for bringing religious values to the workplace to restore harmony. Many companies and labor unions used the guidelines to settle disputes, and the concept gained wide acceptance. The Harvard Business Review described it as "a Magna Carta for management and worker."

From beginning to end, Robert Wood Johnson pursued his dreams with unbridled energy and passion.

Lawrence G. Foster
State College, PA
fosterlg@aol.com

April 2008

"Robert Wood Johnson was one of the twentieth century's most outstanding business executives, and this remarkable book (Robert Wood Johnson: The Gentleman Rebel) gives us fresh insight into a figure whose impact is still very much evident in the business world today."

Professor Richard S. Tedlow, Harvard Business School

Young Robert joins the company

JOINING A YOUNG AND VIBRANT JOHNSON & JOHNSON

When Johnson was sixteen years old, his father died suddenly. A year later he finished Rutgers Prep, and over the objections of his family he decided to forgo college and go to work at Johnson & Johnson with the dream of someday taking his father's place. From an early age he learned from his father the philosophy behind managing the family business.

Robert later warmly recalled his early years in the factory when the Hungarians taught him their skills and became his friends. Hungarians comprised a large part of the work force in the early years of Johnson & Johnson when New Brunswick became a center of life in the United States for immigrants fleeing oppression in their homeland. They were loyal and hard working and quickly befriended young Johnson. "Starting with the first day I went to work, and continuing throughout my business life, I have had many close friends among the Hungarian people in New Brunswick." They would invite him to their homes, to church celebrations, to weddings and christenings; feed him Gulyas, chicken paprika, and Dobos cakes; ply him with wines from Badacsony or Tokaj; and regale him with tales about old Budapest – all to the strains of Gypsy music.

A maturing Bob Johnson had put behind him the carefree, sometimes errant days of frequenting Petey Tennyson's Tavern and was now playing a more urbane role among the young social set in New Brunswick, where again he stood out. His good looks, his wealth, and his family position set him apart from many of the others, and he made no effort to blur these distinctions.

At the factory, though, Johnson was all business. He was always punctual and he worked hard and was learning fast. Still, he had his critics – he always would. His father had chosen and trained a group of serious-minded managers known more for their business acumen than their sentimentality. They were not about to jeopardize their own careers, or the business itself, by hastening the development of the young Johnson, who to many of them was still an unknown factor. Yet they had to deal with the reality of his substantial stock holdings in the company. Some of the managers viewed him with guarded optimism, others with guarded pessimism.

It was in 1915, at the age of twenty-two, that Robert was promoted to his first important position of responsibility, as head of one of the departments in the factory. The workers applauded his promotion, for they considered him one of them.

With the onset of World War I, Robert's responsibilities were greatly increased. The company soon became the major supplier of medical products for all of the Allied Forces, and there was constant pressure from the War Department to keep increasing production. These responsibilities kept him out of military service, and on April 12, 1918, he became General Superintendent in charge of manufacturing when the man who held that position was suddenly taken ill. A few days earlier Robert had turned twenty-five and now owned the large block of company stock left to him by his father.

CREATING THE FAMILY OF COMPANIES

Robert Johnson had set his sights on gaining control of the common shares of the company long before he made those intentions known. He also believed that Johnson & Johnson's destiny would be in his hands as its president, and he was confident of this long before others in the company considered him ready for that position. He had made that determination at the time of his father's death, vowing that someday he would succeed him. Some in the company who had been so worried that Robert would never be successful were now beginning to worry that he would. They saw him as a threat to their own security, and representing a new generation of managers who had both ability and charisma.

As the consumer business continued to grow, Johnson began devoting more of his time and energy to sales and marketing, which he considered his area of strength. Along with this new growth came a concern that the company might lose some of the closeness it had always enjoyed with its employees. Johnson often used the terms "family of companies" and "family of employees," and he believed this spirit was responsible for much of the company's success.

Rapid growth brought another, even more pressing problem. In the aftermath of the war, production continued in high gear as supplies of hospital and consumer products were replenished. But as this tapered off, Johnson and his colleagues began to speculate on where future growth would come from. He later wrote to his uncle, Mead Johnson, "Sometime about 1921, I determined that America was being forced to a policy of isolation and that our export business was about to be destroyed." The answer, he contended, was to begin building an international business based on manufacturing in foreign countries.

EXPANDING AROUND THE WORLD

At the time, there were strong arguments for isolation. Many Americans believed that the country had been drawn into the war needlessly and had paid bitterly. The nation had suffered staggering casualties, and all across America the memorials to the war dead being erected were painful reminders of the cost of becoming involved on foreign soil. A policy of isolation was seen as the only answer – let America take care of America, and let the foreigners take care of the foreigners. Political issues aside, the risks of expanding a business overseas were many, and the rewards were uncertain. The lines were soon drawn, Johnson noted later. He was in favor of establishing manufacturing facilities in international locations, and he was "virtually alone."

In support of his belief that overseas manufacturing should be established, Johnson proposed to the Board of Control, of which he was not yet a member, that he and his brother Seward embark on a worldwide fact-finding trip to confirm the feasibility of the plan. This touched off a heated debate within management that continued for more than a year. Some favored expanding the network of agents and distributors already in place. A few clung to the belief that any international expansion would be inimical to the company's best interests. One or two supported Johnson's position, but not very vocally.

That fall, Johnson again presented to the Board of Control his plan for a fact-finding trip to explore global markets. He later wrote: "Our company needed first-hand information about the chances of doing business in a vast and powerful family of nations spread all over the world. In addition to the British Empire, we need facts on other nations, such as France, China and Japan." The board was not receptive at first, and James Johnson, president of the company, resisted on the grounds that the present export business would be threatened. Finally, the board gave its approval for the trip and after an arduous fact-finding journey around the world, Johnson convinced the board that Johnson & Johnson should become a global company. His foresight in recognizing the potential of global expansion would become a milestone in the company's future business strategy.

BUILDING THE MOST MODERN TEXTILE MILL

Johnson began nurturing new ideas about industry and management that were years ahead of their time. One area that concerned him greatly was that, in the eyes of many, run-down, poorly maintained factories had come to symbolize American industry. Nowhere was this more apparent than in the begrimed textile mills of New England and the South, where working conditions were appalling. In 1926 Johnson decided the company would build the nation's first modern, single-story textile mill on a large tract of land on the outskirts of Gainesville, Georgia. Adjacent to the mill, they would build two hundred modern homes for the mill employees, a grade school, a medical facility, and several churches. Nothing like it had ever been built before, and, when completed, it would revolutionize the construction of textile mills.

Work on the project began immediately. The land site included the watershed of the Chattahoochee River, to ensure a pure water supply for the spinning and weaving operations. The cotton gauze produced at the mill would be sent to New Brunswick to be made into sterile surgical dressings. Built into the sprawling, one-story mill was both technical excellence and an aesthetic beauty that was new to the textile industry. One visiting writer declared: "The plant in Georgia is as nearly perfect as a modern cotton mill could be." Even before its completion it was a showplace that attracted factory and mill designers from all over the world.

In Chicopee Village, as it came to be known, thirty-one variations of modern brick homes were built with three and four bedrooms and laid out on gracefully curved, attractively landscaped streets. Power lines were placed underground, and the homes were among the first in northeastern Georgia to have indoor plumbing, electricity, and hot water. The new mill and the adjoining village changed the lives of those fortunate enough to work and live there.

A PIONEER IN BUILDING MODERN PLANTS

In the years ahead Johnson carried out his "Factories Can Be Beautiful" philosophy by building more than one hundred attractive and efficient plants and office buildings. Others would do the same, but in 1926 he was in the forefront of the concept of modernism that was just beginning to creep into the American consciousness. Not surprisingly, the trend was rebuffed by much of industry, where factories were expected to be "sweatshops" and "salt mines" and where ugly facades hid cluttered, dirty, and unsafe interiors.

From the outset Johnson made it clear that he was not motivated simply by the movement toward modernism. To him, building attractive factories made eminently sound business sense. Attractive factories and pleasant working conditions generated greater efficiency and pride among workers. Well-maintained buildings promoted community acceptance of the company and reflected the integrity of the company and its products. For a company dedicated to purity and sterility in its line of medical products, Johnson believed it made even greater sense. Later he identified what he saw as a still loftier goal: "We build not only structures in which men and women of the future will work, but also the pattern of society in which they will work. We are building frameworks of ideas and ideals."

On February l, 1927, at the age of thirty-three, Robert Johnson was elected to the Board of Control, a key position in the company's hierarchy. His climb from factory hand sixteen years earlier had, for him, been a noble journey. He was no longer the "junior member" of the company. It was the beginning of a new era. Almost immediately he began involving himself in the company's strategic decisions and speaking out on them with authority. And while in some respects he was still the student, he was also the emerging teacher.

Looking to the future of the business, he told them: "We are passing through a time when the management who made this business is letting go of the reins, and the new management is beginning to operate." And, in a not so veiled warning to those who might oppose him, he added: "The stockholders of this business, realizing the necessity for bringing in young men, are also quite ready to sustain the expense of as much of the former organization as is willing to cooperate and help in the progress of Johnson & Johnson."

Neither Johnson nor his management was aware of it at the time, but by cautioning against overproduction he was identifying one of the root causes of the Great Depression that would soon grip the nation. His policy of conserving capital in 1927 had a profound effect on the company's ability to survive the coming economic collapse.

REORGANIZING HOW HOSPITALS ARE STRUCTURED

Although the day-to-day needs of managing the business to cope with the effects of the Depression kept him busy, Johnson continued his visionary approach to health care. Ways to provide better care for hospital patients had challenged his ingenuity since his first exposure to a hospital environment at Middlesex Hospital* nearly fifteen years earlier. For him it was a problem that seemed to defy solution. He could not understand why hospitals were not run more like businesses and less like foundering institutions. Their lack of management appalled him. He had gained a broad understanding of how hospitals in various parts of the world functioned, and in 1931 he outlined what he called "corrective measures" for Middlesex, which for him was a "laboratory" for his hospital reforms. He summarized his suggestions in a report titled "Service to the Patient" and had it printed and distributed. His proposals turned out to be years ahead of their time for general hospitals across the nation.

First, he proposed that the medical staff of the hospital be organized into service departments according to medical specialties – such as, surgery, obstetrics, radiology, gynecology, pediatrics, and pathology. While there was already some specialization at major teaching hospitals, it was years before the larger general hospitals were organized this way, and even longer for smaller hospitals.

BECOMING PRESIDENT AND GENERAL MANAGER

Robert waited a discreet amount of time, and then with little fanfare became President and General Manager of Johnson & Johnson on October 15, 1932, twenty-two years after the death of his father. He had achieved his goal. It had been a long journey to the presidency, but those many years of learning the business and demonstrating his leadership had finally brought its rewards.

---

* Now known as Robert Wood Johnson University Hospital.

Being forty didn't faze Johnson in the slightest; he had always seemed older than his years. He maintained an exhausting work schedule, but always found the time for his many leisure-time pursuits, which included riding his horses, swimming and tennis. He had moved into the company presidency with ease, and his management philosophy was now becoming an integral part of major policy decisions. He continued to push for greater decentralization of Johnson & Johnson operations, which gave smaller units the opportunity to function on their own.

Johnson often recalled the incident that convinced him of the merits of decentralization. An improved formula for making plaster products had been introduced, but some annoying problems had developed in the early production runs. Determined to find the cause, Johnson called a meeting of everyone who had any responsibility for producing the new adhesives, but when seventeen people filed into his office, he was dismayed. "I now know what the problem is," he told them. "Too many people are involved. The meeting is over." Later he assigned one person to be responsible for finding and correcting the problem.

From then on, Johnson was convinced that the best way to run a business was to decentralize it, and that concept evolved into what came to be known as the "Johnson & Johnson Family of Companies." Over time, he became the foremost disciple of decentralized management – and both believing in it and preaching it, he also practiced it ardently. Once a product line was strong enough to support a separate management team, he spun it off and put a separate group in charge.

Another reason he believed in independent units was the human factor, which he later explained in an article in the *Saturday Evening Post*: "Workers need recognition and appreciation," he wrote. "They need to be esteemed in terms of the human equation as well as the production chart." Smaller operations, where more people could be recognized and rewarded, were the answer.

8

The same principles were applied to managing the rapidly expanding global business. First, new product lines were placed with agents. Then, when the business was able to sustain itself, new international affiliates were formed. Once an area of the world demonstrated sufficient growth potential, Johnson was ready to risk putting an affiliate company there, even during the Depression Years – South Africa in 1930, Mexico and Australia in 1931, and Brazil and Argentina later in the 1930s.

A BELIEVER IN "CORPORATE SOCIAL RESPONSIBILITY"

It was more Johnson's philosophy of "corporate social responsibility" than his management style that set him apart from most of the industrialists of his era. In the mid-1930s, when virtually all of American industry was struggling for survival, Johnson came up with the bold concept that business had certain responsibilities toward society and that the more a company lived up to those responsibilities the better sales and profits would be.

The seeds of that belief came in a document he wrote and sent to every major industrialist in the nation in April 1935. He composed the first draft late into several nights, scribbling first the outline and then the text on his favorite lined yellow pads. He titled it "Try Reality." The focus was mainly his arguments on wages and hours, and his suggested solutions to the chaotic economic issues of the day.

Toward the end, however, he delved into what he called his "industrial philosophy" and went on to explain the larger reasons for the very existence of business, beyond merely the goal of making products and profits. These words to the nation's industrial leaders were Johnson's most profound and most prophetic:

> **Out of the suffering of the past few years has been born a public knowledge and conviction that industry only has the right to succeed where it performs a real economic service and is a true social asset.**

> Such permanent success is possible only through the application of an industrial philosophy of enlightened self interest. It is to the enlightened self interest of modern industry to realize that its service to its customers comes first, its service to its employees and management second, and its service to its stockholders last. It is to the enlightened self interest of industry to accept and fulfill its share of social responsibility.

Putting the responsibilities of business in those terms, and linking them to the belief that it was in the enlightened self interest of business to serve customers, employees, and stockholders, in that order, was a new concept for much of American industry to embrace. In many companies the interests of the stockholder reigned supreme. But Johnson saw it differently. "I firmly believe," he later explained, "that if you put the customers, employees and communities (which he added later) first, and you carry out these responsibilities well, then the stockholders will be well served and the company will be successful."

Hoping that the message in "Try Reality" would elicit a groundswell of support from his fellow industrialists, Johnson waited, and waited, in vain. There was no meaningful response, not even at the urgings of the press, as in one editorial: "Mr. Johnson's challenge should not be ignored. He has placed the issue squarely before the nation's industrial leaders. If they continue to evade it in the interest of temporary profits, they can expect nothing but increased taxation and governmental interference with private enterprise."

The rejection by his fellow industrialists did not deter Johnson. Business, he believed, and people like him, were in the seat of power. He told an Associated Press reporter in Atlanta: "America is in the hands of its captains of industry, including all kinds of employers." Nor did his setbacks keep him from being ranked with the nation's business leadership. *Fortune* magazine carried an article and photos of him, oil magnate Jean Paul Getty, and Charles Edison, son of the inventor. And while it took decades to play out, Johnson's philosophy of corporate social responsibility, which he first defined in 1935, was tested and found to have substantial merit.

URGES BUSINESSMEN TO LEARN ABOUT POLITICS

On June 16, Johnson stood before what should have been a hostile audience, the Eighth Annual Institute of Labor at Rutgers University. The assemblage included labor leaders and trade union delegates from the New York metropolitan area and the eastern states. At a time when organized labor was battling to get a toehold in American industry, when issues of the right to collective bargaining and strike-breaking were being settled with bloodied bats, it was not the most promising forum for an industrialist. Congress had finally passed a watered-down bill that was more of an embarrassment to Johnson than to the unions. Already the legal posturing over interpretation of the new 25-cents-an-hour and 44-hour-week limits had begun.

Yet Johnson was philosophical and hopeful. "It is not a good piece of legislation. It is a mighty weak start in a good direction," he told the labor union audience. Then he proceeded to blast labor for failing to support the provisions he had been advocating for years. Their fears that higher wages and shorter hours would make unions unnecessary, he said, were totally unfounded. He also had some advice: "You have not been able to sell the principle of organized labor to the underpaid worker in the past fifty years; you will raise the potential number of union members a thousandfold by establishing decent maximum hours and minimum wages." Later in the speech, he made what many considered a shrewd observation: "American businessmen," he said, "are probably the most efficient in the world, but I am afraid they are nevertheless political morons. I find we have as astute a group of politicians as we have anywhere, but I am afraid they are business morons. But there are more politicians who know something about business than there are businessmen who know something about politics."

The news wires hummed with that quote, which was covered as a story on its own. "The ovation at the end was without parallel," one reporter wrote.

A LESSON IN SOCIAL RESPONSIBILITY

Johnson had spoken before many audiences in the past several years, most of them representing business, labor, and politics. On January 6, 1939, he went to Athens, Georgia, to address the student body at the University of Georgia, not far from where he had built the world's most modern textile mill. Some of his mill workers were the parents of students who gathered in the university chapel to hear him speak.

"If business leadership will assume their full social responsibility, I have no fear for the economic progress of our country," he told them. "It is the job of modern management to give the people they employ a full sense of security growing out of accomplishment and performance, as well as a declaration of purpose." Otherwise, he said, "no management is worthy of its position."

"Business has missed the greatest opportunity of the century," he continued. "Industrial leaders have largely ignored the negative public attitude toward management. Let business conduct itself in the community in which it operates so as to win the approval and the confidence of its neighbors. If this is done, we will not require any of the national business organizations which are said to speak for business. They have accomplished exactly nothing."

A VERY GENEROUS PERSON

By nature, Johnson was a very generous person. Some of his colleagues thought he might be too generous. "If you didn't watch him, he would give away the factory," one commented. Just before Christmas in 1936 he took 12,000 shares of his Johnson & Johnson stock (then a privately owned company) and formed the Johnson New Brunswick Foundation. This later became the

Robert Wood Johnson Foundation, and with $1.2 billion from Johnson's estate it became the nation's largest philanthropy devoted to improving health care in America.

The Foundation's early focus was on the people of New Brunswick, many of whom were still feeling the effects of the Depression. Johnson had always felt an allegiance to the place where he was born and where the company had its origins, so when word got out that he had formed a foundation, the requests for assistance began pouring in. There was no pattern of giving. The help ranged from food and clothing for poor families, to fixing an orphan boy's teeth before he departed for Boy's Town in Nebraska, to a down payment on a house for a highly regarded Black policeman with a wife and eight children. As long as the dividends from the stock held out, the needy were seldom turned away, and when they were depleted, Johnson dug into his own pocket to help.

His abiding interest in improving health care prompted Johnson to refocus the Foundation's various projects at the two New Brunswick hospitals, Middlesex and St. Peter's. Concerned about increasing the flow of physicians, Johnson had the Foundation provide no-interest loans to a large number of young men from New Brunswick who wanted to become doctors but could not afford a medical school education. They agreed to repay the loans when they established themselves in practice, but very few of them ever did, and this was always a great disappointment to him.

THE NEW CHAIRMAN OF THE BOARD

On May 17, 1938, Johnson announced to his Board of Directors, all of whom were members of management in the privately held company, that he was becoming the company's first Chairman of the Board. "I shall not work any less," he told them. "I am merely putting the New Brunswick plant under independent management, just as the other companies of the firm have been for the past ten years." He was now forty-five years old, and since he

13

had taken over management of the company, annual sales had increased from $18 million to $33 million.

Whether he held the title of President or Chairman made little difference to the outside world. True, he was backed by a superb management team that ran the day-to-day operations, but Robert Johnson *was* Johnson & Johnson, and it would be that way for the twenty-five years he was Chairman.

JOHNSON THE PATRIOT CALLED TO DUTY

Early on the morning of December 7, 1941, the Japanese attacked Pearl Harbor, inflicting shocking losses and throwing the nation into a frenzy. The next day, Congress approved a declaration of war on Japan, and three days later the United States was at war with Germany and Italy as well. Defense preparation suddenly became wartime reality, and citizens throughout the land – men, women, and children – sought to aid the cause in whatever ways they could. It was a time for mobilizing patriotism as well as arms.

On December 19, New Jersey Governor Charles Edison called Johnson to Trenton, explained the urgent need to establish a rationing program for civilians, and asked him to become New Jersey's rationing administrator. He accepted, on condition that he be allowed to resign if a more vital assignment in the war effort came later. The governor agreed.

In the following months, he handled the rationing job with crisp efficiency, a reflection of his ability to organize and keep things as simple as possible. Meanwhile, he made inquiries about entering Army service, and there was immediate interest – based on his business record and his demonstrated skills as an executive.

On April 21, 1942, Johnson submitted his resignation to Governor Edison, saying that he would be commissioned as an Army colonel on May 4. He was to report to the Army Ordnance Department in Washington, the group responsible for providing all military supplies, but first he made a hasty trip to Michigan to inspect the new plant of Midland Ordnance Foundation Inc., which Johnson & Johnson had set up as a nonprofit subsidiary to do war work, principally as a shell-loading depot.

SMALL BUSINESS NEEDED HELP TO SURVIVE

Small businesses in America were hurting because most of the war contracts were going to large companies, which were capable of producing the vast quantities of goods needed for the war. However, some 165,000 businesses in the "small company" category were desperately in need of war contracts to ensure their survival, since most of them had been cut off from raw materials that were being diverted to the war effort. The government enlisted the services of Wall Street wizard Floyd Odlum and gave him an opportunity to deal with the problem, but he quit in disgust when he learned it was just an advisory role. Congress tried several times to come up with a solution before creating the Smaller War Plants Corporation, which had a $150 million budget for loans to help conversions to wartime production.

Three weeks after arriving in Washington, Johnson was summoned to the Shoreham Hotel to meet with Donald M. Nelson, chairman of the War Production Board, who told him President Roosevelt wanted him to take over the Smaller War Plants Corporation. "I hesitated, and finally declined," Johnson said later. "I felt committed to the Ordnance Department. I thought my experience was more appropriate to the procurement services than to the role of remedying what seemed to me, all things considered, a hopeless situation."

On June 25 a column in the *Washington Daily News* said: "President Roosevelt wants his good and liberal friend, Robert Johnson, head of a big pharmaceutical firm, named chief of the War Production Board's new Smaller War Plants Corporation. But certain WPB bigshots are trying to sabotage the appointment. And certain Congressmen too. Mr. Johnson is a Big Business Man. They want a Little Business Man."

15

The inference was clear enough. The "big" and "little" had to do with whether he would be too independent for the bureaucrats to handle, not with the size of the business Johnson ran. Roosevelt wanted that kind of independence, but others saw Johnson as a loose cannon on deck.

That September, Johnson was transferred to New York City to become chief of the New York Ordnance District, where he had a staff of 2,800 and directed purchasing from some 7,000 manufacturers in the metropolitan area. Very little was being purchased from small businesses. On October 14, Johnson was summoned to Washington to appear before the Senate Committee on Problems of Small Business Enterprises. The fact that he was the first witness suggested that the committee had heard from the White House.

With his usual confidence, Johnson told the Senate committee he had the solution: "There is only one way that small business could be systematically built into the war effort, and that is to decentralize procurement services and establish regional offices in every major city, to act as liaison with local manufacturers, and to nurse them into the war effort."

By the end of 1942, the Smaller War Plants Corporation had managed to place only 224 contracts totaling just over $9 million with small companies. With some 120,000 small companies on the verge of bankruptcy, the situation was critical.

Early in January 1943, Johnson was ordered to report to Washington for a new assignment. He went straight to the White House for an urgent meeting, where he was told that President Roosevelt wanted him to take over the Smaller War Plants Corporation. This time there was no refusing it. "I certainly did not want the job," Johnson recalled, "but I took it." On January 19 the White House announced Johnson's appointment as Vice Chairman of the War Production Board (WPB) and Chairman of the Smaller War Plants Corporation (SWPC).

TRUCE WITH HARRY S. TRUMAN

Though most members of Congress were anxious to approve Johnson's appointment and send him into the fray carrying the banner for small business, there was some resounding vocal opposition. One of the shrillest outcries came from the Democratic Senator from Missouri, Harry S. Truman, who asked publicly how someone as closely identified with big business as Johnson was could possibly represent the interests of small business. Later Johnson revealed that he had visited Truman personally and offered to resign if the senator ever found any conflict between his industrial position and the new appointment. After the two men met, Truman withdrew his objections and the appointment was approved.

Johnson took over the SWPC on February 8, a job that Washington columnist Drew Pearson called "the most difficult, undesirable job in government." The *Chicago Tribune* described it as a "hot seat." From the beginning, Johnson displayed a certain bravado and arrogance about the assignment that won him both praise and condemnation. He already had a penchant for making bold comments to the press, which were quickly transmitted into bold headlines. His most recent daring and imprudent statement came when he told a reporter that he had given himself just six months to do the job – the job that most people in Washington considered impossible. "If I don't do it in that time, they'll get rid of me, and if I do it by that time they'll also get rid of me, because the job will be done." The United Press carried the story across the nation to the believers and the doubters, many of whom were in Washington, including some of Johnson's superiors in the Army.

The announcement of Johnson's appointment came directly from the White House instead of through regular channels. *Barron's* reported that this was done in order to give the "errant ·colonel" some needed clout with his Army superiors and the War Production Board. From the outset, Johnson missed no opportunity to annoy his Army superiors, to the delight of leaders in Congress, the press, and the droves of hopeful small businessmen waiting to be rescued. At one of his first press conferences, he was asked whether he was an Army officer or an executive of the War Production Board. He replied, "I am responsible only to Donald Nelson (Chairman of the WPB), and through him to Congress. I am not responsible to anyone else." That rankled the brass at the Pentagon.

"Rarely can an Army officer affront his superiors and get away with it," said *Barron's*, but Johnson got the SWPC job primarily because influential congressmen were burning to 'save' their business constituents and Johnson was the one official who had said, with table-pounding aggressiveness, that they could be saved."

Johnson began by seeking autonomy for the SWPC and outlined what he saw at stake. One of his most persuasive arguments came in a letter to New York's Governor Thomas E. Dewey, who was then grappling with a string of small-plant bankruptcies in his state. Johnson wrote: "If we are going to lose in this war the advantages of private enterprise and the enthusiasm that grows out of owner-management, we are going to lose one of the most important ingredients of production, besides losing the American way of life." Dewey made the letter public and it drew wide attention.

Nothing had worked so far, so it was up to WPC Chairman Nelson to take drastic action. He was acutely aware of the growing pressure from Congress and the White House on the War Production Board to take corrective action. Carter Brooke Jones of the *Washington Star* disclosed on March 23 that Nelson had quietly signed an order giving the SWPC complete authority over its own activities.

Now it was up to Johnson. Announcing that he had a plan, he said he would focus first on pulling together what he called "the greatest collection of buying-power ever generated in the United States to a given program." Then he would decentralize into regions and bring distressed companies face to face with those who had production orders, not only military procurement

18

officers but also the big corporations and local and state government agencies that bought supplies. Then he would recruit experienced businessmen to volunteer their services as intermediaries until all the distressed companies were finally back to work. He was absolutely convinced the plan would work. "For good or evil," he declared dramatically, "I am proceeding with my plan."

TUMULTUOUS DAYS IN WASHINGTON

When Johnson got frustrated over the amount of correspondence it took to answer one question in government, he put all the letters on one issue on a scale, had a photo taken, and got it printed in the newspapers. This upset Harry Truman, among others.

Though the decision to focus on the regional boards was made for operational reasons, it became an enormous political advantage to the SWPC. Now when congressmen came crying for help for distressed plants in their districts, they were referred to the regional board run by their own constituents. By deflecting the problem away from Washington and back to the local level, Congress was off the hook. Johnson hadn't planned it that way, but it was, in the words of Ward Schultz of the *Detroit Times*, a "ten strike."

ROOSEVELT NAMES RWJ GENERAL

The White House had been carefully monitoring Johnson's progress at the SWPC and was aware of his handicap. As a colonel, he had little hope of pulling rank in a wartime Washington that had an abundance of military brass. Roosevelt decided to correct that, and on May 17, the White House announced that the president was naming Johnson a Brigadier General of Army Ordnance. Immediately, eyebrows were raised all over Washington, especially beneath the braided caps at the Pentagon. It was rare for an Army promotion to be announced by the White House. Roosevelt was sending out a clear but unspoken message about the standing of the man he had put in charge of the SWPC – that he was not to be taken lightly at the Pentagon and that he would have presidential backing.

The promotion suited Johnson fine. General Robert Wood Johnson. It sounded much better than "Colonel." Little did he realize that he would be a general for exactly sixty-four days.

The military uniform was important to Johnson. It always had been, even during his prep school days when he was elected captain of the Company B Drill Team and wore the snappy military uniform with a wide-brim campaign hat. Military uniforms, for Johnson, were not clothing but a costume worn by another personality within himself. He was a meticulous dresser – his clothes did not hang on him, they were sculptured. The tailoring was flawless, the standards having been set by the dedicated needle-wielders in the custom shops along Oxford Street in London many years earlier. And wherever he went, he pursued the same standards of sartorial perfection.

He had an Italian tailor custom-make his colonel's uniform, and he brought him back for the new fittings. They were tediously long, but for this purpose he had infinite patience. The results were impressive. He was slender, and he had a ramrod military posture. There was no better-fitting military wardrobe in Washington.

As brigadier general he began an exhaustive travel schedule to meet with his regional boards. Quietly, he had supplemented his staff by recruiting a number of senior-level business executives – some from his own company – to contribute their time as "unofficial volunteers at $1 a year."

JOHNSON'S PROGRAM SHOWS PROGRESS

Despite the frustrations, some positive things began to happen. Over a seven-week period that summer, the SWPC placed orders with small businesses for 2,625 prime contracts valued at $217 million. Among the companies were 1,285 that had not previously received war work. One problem with reporting on progress was the tediously slow system that was in place. Months elapsed before new gains were made public. It was a start, but it was only a fraction of the billions in contracts Johnson had so intemperately promised.

Johnson then began crossing swords with members of the War Production Board, where he was vice chairman. In a speech before the New York Advertising Club, he said that war production had been delayed some six months by the erection of new plants that were not needed. "We have made mistakes," he declared. "We built new plants, big ones and too many. We built facilities that existed across the street." The "we" meant "they," since Johnson had never participated in those decisions. In the eyes of his Washington critics he was becoming increasingly dangerous, yet his candor continued to win him new admirers.

By early summer 1943, the tide of battle in Europe was beginning to turn in favor of the Allies. The Nazis had lost in Africa, were losing the Battle of the Atlantic, and were suffering huge losses in Allied air strikes. In the United States there was cautious talk that the end of the war in Europe was in sight.

Planning the transition of industrial production from wartime to peacetime took on a greater importance. Johnson and others began to focus on releasing increased quantities of scarce but non-critical materials to small companies so they could begin their recovery. The concept gained immediate appeal, because for some companies it was their only hope of survival. But the more Johnson tried to negotiate the transition, the more he was rebuffed by the military brass. The tension grew.

RESIGNS HIS SWPC POST IN WASHINGTON

For someone who doted so on being well organized, Johnson's life had fallen into disarray. Between waging the battle of Washington and dealing with the changes in his personal life, he had worn himself to a frazzle, physically and emotionally. His march on Washington and the bureaucracy was now about over. It had been neither a supreme victory nor a crushing defeat. He had focused national attention on the plight of small businesses and diverted substantial war work their way, but he fell far short of the billions in war contracts he had promised in the early days as chairman of the SWPC. He never came close to that goal.

On September 16 the *Washington Star* speculated that he was about to resign as chairman of the Smaller War Plants Corporation: "Johnson recently went to the Cornell Medical Clinic for a check-up," the paper reported. "As a result of that his doctors advised that he would have to 'slow down.' He was in Washington today for a meeting of regional chiefs of SWPC and will return to the clinic for further tests." Eight days later, on September 24, Johnson called a press conference and announced he was stepping down as SWPC chairman because of poor health. "The corporation's work is now in hand," he said. That was only partially true, as subsequent press assessment would show.

His parting words were picked up by Walter Winchell and newspapers all across the nation. "Washington," Johnson said, "is a magnet for mediocrity."

A MIXED REACTION TO HIS ACCOMPLISHMENTS

The comment stirred up even more debate about Johnson in Washington. There were sharply divergent views on why he had quit and how effective he had been while there. Johnson summed up his side of the debate in a letter to New Jersey Governor Edison: "The job was in hand, the organization was complete, the policies were established, and the house was in order. There was no widespread destitution in small business in America, and I had suffered a physical collapse, which for the first time in my life has put me out of circulation. These are the reasons; there are no others."

But *Business Week* magazine had a different view of why he left Washington: "Johnson's temerity in suggesting that as ordnance contracts are cut back the Army should release the materials for essential civilian uses so incensed Robert P. Patterson, Under Secretary of War, and Lt. Gen. Brehon B.

Somervell, chief of the Army Service Forces, that they prevailed upon Donald Nelson as chairman of WPB to request Johnson's resignation. Just a few weeks previously Johnson had resigned his wartime commission as brigadier general to do battle for civilian industry without the restraint laid upon him by his uniform. And Johnson's parting shot when he quit SWPC was that more orderly administration of the home front would be one of the greatest contributions to the war effort. Pointing a finger at absenteeism, he said that when women have to stay home to do the family washing, a washing machine becomes as important as a bomber."

No one could argue that Johnson's health might have been sufficient reason for him to leave Washington when he did, but there was little support for his contention that small business was on the road to recovery, to the extent that he said it was. It would take the termination of the war, still nearly two years away, for small business to really begin its revitalization. So the suspicion lingered that Johnson had been ambushed by a group that didn't think mavericks made good Army generals on the battlefields of Washington.

THANKS FROM PRESIDENT ROOSEVELT

Among the first letters he received expressing regret over his illness and resignation was one from President Roosevelt, written on September 28:

> Dear Bob,
> I am awfully sorry to have you leave. You have done grand work and I hope much that you will really take care of yourself and get well quickly. When you get about again, run in and see me.
> Always sincerely,
FDR

One senior staff member of the SWPC wrote him:

> Dear Mr. Johnson:
> This place seems like a morgue since you left. Everyone would be most happy to have you return, health permitting.

These were not the sentiments at the Pentagon, where they were happy to be rid of him.

BIRTH OF THE CREDO

During his recuperation after leaving Washington, Johnson went to New Brunswick only once, on December 12, 1943, for a Board of Directors meeting. That day he announced that in 1944 Johnson & Johnson would become a publicly held company. All the members of the Board held senior management positions in the company, and they welcomed the news that they would soon become stockholders. Christmas came early that year. Johnson, of course, would continue to be the major stockholder. Years earlier he had added to his already significant holdings when he bought most of the stock owned by his sister, Evangeline.

Johnson emphasized to the Board that the company's management philosophy would not change under public ownership. He outlined the four areas of responsibility that the company would continue to follow:

> The first concern should be to provide the consuming public with goods of the highest quality at the lowest possible prices.
> Next in importance is the maintenance of full employment at a fair scale of wages.
> Third, there should be adequate executive compensation to assure the corporation of the most efficient management available.
> Fourth, we must have adequate return on the capital invested by the stockholders, with emphasis on the maintenance of an adequate cash position, enabling the corporation to take advantage of every opportunity for the profitable development and expansion of its business.

These were the same areas Johnson had introduced in 1935 and tried, unsuccessfully, to get other corporations to adopt. They would also become the core of the Johnson & Johnson "Credo," which he would write and introduce in the coming year.

WELCOME HOME, GENERAL

It soon became evident that the title "General" would have a far longer life span than his Army commission did. He would become "General" to all but his most intimate friends and close family – to them he remained "Bob." There were some exceptions: his old cronies from the early days and a few of the senior mill workers who had helped shepherd him through his errant youth. A few persisted in calling him "Bob," and when he strode through the mill an occasional daring "Bobby" could be heard, usually from one of the Hungarian old-timers.

Once, in later years, he mused about people addressing him as "General," contending that he had taken a neutral position. He said those who wanted to call him "General" could, and those who didn't need not. He made it sound a great deal more discretionary than it actually was. It is not surprising that almost everyone called him "General." Actually, "General" fit him quite well – a custom fit – and there was no question that he was again in command of the home forces.

Whenever he came back to the office after an absence, everyone was ready for his inevitable inspection. For weeks before, it was customary to apply paint and polish liberally to any area of the office or factory that might not pass his close scrutiny. His obsession with neatness and cleanliness was by now widely known, and feared. Nothing could arouse him quicker than even the slightest evidence of poor housekeeping. To him a smudge was tantamount to treason. He claimed that a medical products company should always glisten, especially one that claimed a state of sterility for many of its products. He was right and they knew it.

JOHNSON THE AUTHOR EMERGES

As the demands of the war had increased, the business had accelerated to a frenetic pace, so it was not difficult for him to rationalize that he was needed. And even though the company was in the process of going public, he still saw it as "his" company – in terms of responsibility for its welfare.

The book he had been writing about his Washington episode had kept him busy and rekindled the constant desire he had to write. A few weeks before he returned to the office, he completed it, and then arranged to have the manuscript edited. He submitted the final version to the Princeton University Press, which published it several months later. The 150-page volume was titled *"But, General Johnson – "* *Episodes in a War Effort*, which mimicked the response he said he had often received: "But, General Johnson, it can't be done."

He was honest about the effort. In a cover note to business associates and friends who received copies, he called the book "something of a hodgepodge." But as readers discovered, it was more than that. In the preface, Johnson expressed his objective and hope for the book:

> . . . American small business is only a segment of the national environment, but it touches every phase of American life. To explore the public efforts to solve its problems in a war economy is to obtain an insight into modern government which, with understanding, may lead to progress, but which without understanding, will foster despair.

He then proceeded to describe, honestly and with a touch of humor, his Washington experiences in behalf of small business, drawing on newspaper reports and congressional testimony to support his views.

HIS SPIRIT OF PATRIOTISM RAN DEEP

The spirit of patriotism ran deep in Johnson. He openly expressed love of country, flag, and democracy, and never missed an opportunity to reaffirm these beliefs. The roving nature of *"But, General Johnson"* gave him the latitude to challenge Americans to pay closer attention to their civic duties. He reminded them that they were allowing the national news media to "make up the mind of America on the great issues of the day" because they had failed to exercise their voting privileges:

> American democracy has been down on one knee for a quarter of a century. It has been knocked there by Americans. The Americans who do not vote in the primary elections. The Americans who do not vote in general elections. The Americans who do not vote at all.
>
> Our democracy is based on the principle that we shall have a government of amateurs, not professionals. It is built on the belief that an everyday citizen will run for office and be aggressively supported by everyday citizens – his friends and followers. The idea of leaving government to professionals is not American – and it is not safe.
>
> The men coming back from our fighting fronts will be in no mood to be pushed around by bureaucrats and sub-bureaucrats. They will want, above everything, freedom of action. Freedom to work. Freedom to live their own lives. Freedom to succeed.

In the final chapter Johnson looked to the future, and it was here that the visionary businessman emerged, in an element he knew and understood well. "The time has come to look ahead," he wrote. "A reconversion period is upon us. It is no longer only a question of helping small business. It is even more than a 'transition' to a peace economy. *It is a matter of maintaining independent business as a permanent part of the industrial structure.*"

INTRODUCTION OF THE CREDO

Johnson then presented for the first time his enlarged version of the corporate responsibility statement he had introduced in 1935 in the "Try Reality" document. Entitled "An Industrial Credo," it spelled out a company's responsibilities to customers, employees, management, and stockholders, in that order:

AN INDUSTRIAL CREDO

We believe that our *first* responsibility is to our Customers –
Our products must always be good, and
We must strive to make them better at lower costs.
Our orders must be promptly and accurately filled.
Our dealers must make a fair profit.

Our *second* responsibility is to those who work with us – the Men and Women in our Factories and Offices –
They must have a sense of security in their jobs.
Wages must be fair and adequate,
Management just,
Hours short, and
Working conditions clean and orderly.
Workers should have an organized system for suggestions and complaints.
Foremen and department heads must be qualified and fair-minded.
There must be opportunity for advancement – for those qualified – and
Each person must be considered an individual standing on his own dignity and merit.

Our *third* responsibility is to our Management –
Our executives must be persons of talent, education, experience, and ability.
They must be persons of common sense and full understanding.

Our *fourth* and last responsibility is to our Stockholders –
    Business must make a sound profit.
    Reserves must be created,
    Research must be carried on,
    Adventurous programs developed, and
    Mistakes made and paid for.
    Bad times must be provided for,
    High taxes paid,
    New machines purchased,
    New factories built,
    New products launched, and
    New sales plans developed.
    We must experiment with new ideas.
    When these things have been done, the stockholder
    should receive a fair return.
    We are determined, with the help of God's Grace, to
    fulfill these obligations to the best of our ability.

THE HEART OF JOHNSON & JOHNSON'S CULTURE

Shortly after the Credo appeared in the book, hundreds of copies were printed and distributed throughout the company, and framed copies began appearing on the walls of company offices all over the world. Beginning with the company's Board of Directors, Johnson declared that henceforth the principles set forth in the Credo would be the company's philosophy. Those who did not endorse it could look for employment elsewhere. The Credo became the heart of Johnson & Johnson's culture and guided its destiny from then on.

When critics quickly pointed out that it was not realistic to place the stockholders last, Johnson disagreed vehemently. "If we put the customer first and follow through on our other responsibilities, I assure you that the stockholders will be well served," he would say, and sometimes add, "And, don't forget, I am the largest stockholder."

Johnson & Johnson did become a publicly held company in 1944, and the wisdom of Johnson's philosophy would become dramatically clear. The initial offering price of a share of stock was $37.50. An investor who purchased one hundred shares for $3,750 in 1944 and held the stock would see it grow, with stock splits, to 124,848 shares valued at about $12 million by 2007, not counting dividends.

CORPORATE RESPONSIBILITY MEANT TAKING ACTION

Writing about corporate responsibility was not as important as taking action, Johnson believed. Of all the concepts embodied in his Credo, none became more visible to the general public than his "Factories Can Be Beautiful" concept. It had its origins with the first modern textile mill and 150-home village he built in Georgia in 1927. In the ensuing years, Johnson guided the construction of more than one hundred trend-setting plants and office buildings throughout the world. Many were unique and years ahead of their time.

In the late 1930s, Johnson had developed a formula for the results he wanted to achieve. Earlier, in 1934, he surprised everyone by calling in the widely heralded architectural firm of Shreve, Lamb & Harmon, which had recently completed work on the dramatic new 102-story Empire State Building in New York City. Having designed the world's tallest skyscraper, the architects were somewhat nonplussed to find that what Johnson had in mind was a one-story building. He wanted it to be expandable in all four directions and to utilize aluminum and plastic and other new building materials. Not satisfied with the initial design, he modified it with the help of his own construction staff.

When the pace of construction picked up in later years, the Johnson & Johnson plants became widely known for innovation. Virtually all the new factories were located on large tracts of land, often on hundreds of acres. Johnson believed that a company's manufacturing site could be as attractive as a college campus. Close attention was given to landscaping. That was a Johnson rule. He believed the new buildings should blend into the setting and be an asset to the community.

Johnson had a hand in the design and construction of every plant and made frequent visits to the construction sites to make sure the buildings were developing as he had anticipated. The changes he ordered drove the architects and builders to the brink of despair, but no one argued with the results. The facades of the buildings were all different – the most talked about was in marble and all had clean lines and were superbly functional. Vast expanses of tinted glass made it possible for workers to look out and enjoy the pastoral setting. The plush lobbies and reception areas resembled movie sets, some with floor-to-ceiling windows, velvet drapes, and recessed lighting. And, to promote the feeling that it was their plant, employees were encouraged to use the lobby entrances.

Manufacturing areas were bright and airy and often air-conditioned. The walls were pastel-colored, as were the specially designed covers that shielded the moving parts of all production machinery. These covers kept oily bearings from soiling the white nurse-type uniforms that had been the traditional wear for women employees since the company's earliest days. There were strict rules regarding housekeeping, and heads would roll when they were violated.

NEITHER CONSERVATIVE NOR LIBERAL

When asked why he went to great expense to build plants of this quality, Johnson had a ready answer. In the long run, he said, they were less expensive. His employees took pride in their workplace, and morale was high – ensuring greater output and higher-quality products. What's more, the plants were an asset to the community. All of this might have been lost if the company had lower standards.

But the concepts and philosophy introduced in the Credo in *"But, General Johnson"* captured the most attention and comment. He had sent the book to an extensive list of industrial leaders, political figures, educators, and journalists, and it was reviewed in the *New York Times Book Review* and numerous other newspapers.

All found some merit in what he had to say. The *Times* reviewer, Walter T. Beachboard, agreed with some of his recommendations but labeled him as "a true business liberal," which brought a prompt reply from Johnson: "Most of us feel that we can move toward better times if we can combine the merits of the Old Deal with the merits of the New Deal," he wrote. "It is unfortunate that our people are so tightly locked in camps. . . . I am for taking the good out of each and developing a postwar pattern that can be an improvement over the past."

By contrast, the reviewer for the *St. Louis Post-Dispatch*, Henry B. Kline, while agreeing with some of Johnson's views, saw him as a conservative who "somewhat resembles the enlightened conservatism of Eric Johnson and *Fortune* magazine."

That happened often. Many people had difficulty putting a label on Johnson because his philosophy embraced both conservative and liberal views, depending on how they were being applied. It was impossible to stamp him as one or the other. And while some saw this as contradictory, he did not. The confusion, he felt, rested not with him but with those whose vision was limited. He saw the wisdom of examining all sides of an issue.

THE WAR WAS OVER BUT NOT AT HOME

By the middle of 1944, a growing confidence in ultimate victory both in Europe and in the Pacific began taking hold in America. Rome became the first European capital to be recaptured after Allied forces fought their way from Anzio Beach. Following the massive landing at Normandy, the invasion of Europe from the west was under way. And American forces were rapidly changing the course of the war in the Pacific. At home, Franklin D. Roosevelt won a historic fourth term as President, with Harry S. Truman as his running mate, by a heavy electoral vote but a much narrower popular majority over Governor Thomas E. Dewey of New York.

When the outcome of the war no longer seemed in doubt, Americans began to devote increasing attention and concern to the formidable problems that would accompany conversion to a peacetime economy. There were fears that the winding down of the spectacular surge of wartime production would result in a dramatic collapse of the economy. And those who had vivid memories of the painful Great Depression and its record unemployment and bread lines worried the most. The war had brought management and labor together to fight the common enemy and preserve liberty, but peacetime positioning would once again be dominated by divergent interests.

On the afternoon of April 12, 1945, at the Little White House at Warm Springs, Georgia, President Roosevelt died of a massive cerebral hemorrhage at age sixty-three. Three hours later Vice President Truman took the oath as the nation's thirty-second President. Three weeks later, Germany surrendered unconditionally, bringing the war in Europe to an end. Then, on August 14, the Japanese surrendered unconditionally. A week earlier the first atomic bomb, equal to 20,000 tons of TNT, had been dropped on Hiroshima, followed by another unleashed on Nagasaki two days later.

RETURN TO WASHINGTON WITH A FORCEFUL MESSAGE

It had been nearly two years since Johnson's abrupt departure from Washington, and in the fall of 1945 he returned, in the familiar but still controversial role of an industrialist urging Congress to increase the national minimum wage. This time there was new tension surrounding that sensitive issue, but again Johnson volunteered to enter the fray. He had espoused the cause of higher wages so often and under such hostile circumstances that by now no one doubted the sincerity of his motives, though some questioned the wisdom of his actions.

But this time the wage issue had a new backdrop. During the war, strikes had been forbidden and national loyalty and pride kept the labor force producing at peak levels. But many months before the Japanese armistice, when the outcome of the war became a virtual certainty, labor unions began positioning themselves for their role in the reconversion to peace. The transition was not as smooth as had been anticipated, and with each new labor demand for wage increases came the threat of strikes and discord. The Labor Department and the War Labor Board tried hard to maintain stability, but it was like trying to contain a prairie fire driven by a brisk breeze.

Hope of hearing more from business in favor of a higher minimum wage was all but lost. Proponents of the bill had invited Johnson to testify, but still bearing some of the scars of his earlier battles, he took quite a while to make up his mind to return to Washington. At 10 o'clock on the morning of October 23, however, with shoulders squared and that familiar glint in his eye, he strode into Room 424B in the Senate Office Building to testify.

It was memorable, even by Washington congressional committee hearing standards. Johnson's opening remarks characterized the hearings as a discussion on "the plight of the underpaid," and then, having set the stage, he proceeded to jolt even the liberal-minded senators with his recommendation.

"I suggest," he said in a clear, forceful voice, "that the committee should take the position that the average American workman cannot keep body and soul together on less than $30 per week anywhere in the United States. On the basis of a 40-hour week, I, therefore, am compelled to recommend a 75 cents an hour wage throughout the nation."

Committee members looked at one another in dismay. The bill called for an increase from 40 to 65 cents an hour, and Johnson was proposing 75 cents an hour. The rebel industrialist had returned.

URGES "NEW CODE OF BUSINESS ETHICS" FOR THE NATION

Johnson then took his argument to an even loftier plane: "What we are really doing is *creating a new code of business ethics* with the aid and guidance of our federal government. It would be hard to imagine a more important task, nor one that would make a greater contribution to the world." The senators listened intently. "It was the underpaid, the unemployed, and the destitute of Europe," Johnson continued, "that caused the political upheavals which led to this great war. . . . We have come to a time we can honestly say, at least in our country, that man does not have the right to employ his fellow man unless he can pay a subsistence wage."

It was a moving speech, and the hearing room stirred uneasily when he concluded. No one had ever defined the minimum-wage issue in quite those terms before.

The following day, beginning with headlines across the nation, Johnson's presentation received wide coverage, and it was generally highly favorable to his proposals. Editorial support followed, and magazine coverage was equally encouraging. A *Time* magazine article in the November 5 issue gave the story a man-bites-dog twist:

> When a businessman demands that labor get more pay for less work, that's news. Last week a big businessman made such news by telling Congress: the U.S. should boost the legal minimum wage from 40 cents an hour to a minimum of 75¢. At the same time, he recommended that Congress prepare legislation to establish a 40, a 36 and a 30-hour week. Commerce, industry, the trades and agriculture would be classified into three major divisions and three work weeks. But all would get the same weekly minimum wage, $30.
>
> This suggestion came from dapper, poker-faced Robert Wood Johnson, 53, wartime brigadier general (in Ordnance and as boss of the Smaller War Plants Corp.) and board chairman of Johnson & Johnson (surgical supplies). To a Senate labor subcommittee, now considering a bill to raise the minimum to 65¢ an hour,

Johnson said: "not high enough; the U.S. can now pay higher wages and sell at lower costs."

Bob Johnson's best argument was his own company. It now has the highest minimum wage in the industry. Average hourly earnings for day work, excluding overtime and premiums, are 76¢ for women and 85¢ for men, while piecework rates run higher. In his southern textile mills Johnson pays a minimum now of 65¢ – at least 10¢ higher than competitors. Anticipating critics who would not fail to point out that he does not practice what he preaches, Johnson said that he would be glad to pay more if competitors were forced to do the same.

PRESS CALLED HIM "HERO OF THE WORKING CLASS"

The press continued to hail him as a hero of the working class, some members of Congress wrote letters of support, there was a flurry of encouraging mail from businessmen, and one company launched an advertising campaign on behalf of the plan. Chester Bowles, head of the Office of Price Administration, went before the same Senate committee to give his support to Johnson.

For a while there was hope that the Johnson plan might be embraced. Then critics of the proposal, led by major industrialists and the conservative factions in Congress, began their counterarguments. Johnson had heard all the rebuttals before, but this time he hoped that with the end of the war, sentiments would change. Getting decent jobs for returning servicemen and women had been given top priority by many, and here was a chance to act on that promise. But no. All the arguments that had historically been raised against increasing the minimum wage were brought up again. Even Johnson's most convincing argument – It is much cheaper to increase wages and create more buying power than it is to pay for putting people on the welfare rolls – stirred no outpouring of support from business in general. More frustrating for Johnson were the large numbers of businessmen and legislators who remained stonily silent, preferring to avoid the delicate issue – the safer course. Labor, naturally, agreed with Johnson.

JOHNSON THE WRITER TAKES ON THE PRESS

Johnson's management philosophy had been receiving much wider attention during the previous two years because of the articles he was writing for major magazines, such as the *Saturday Evening Post*. Writing had always held a particular fascination for him. It was a way of expressing his ideas. The publication of *"But, General Johnson"* had brought a flurry of praise, some polite and some sincere, and it offered him further encouragement. The timing was right, for in the mid-1940s many of the leading magazines were eager to publish by-line articles by well-known businessmen who had something to say, especially if it was controversial. In this role, Johnson was a natural.

His approach to what some saw as the "writing phase" of his life was similar to the way he undertook any other new subject – he sought help from the experts. At the time, it was common practice for experienced journalists and authors to provide help, for a fee, to businessmen and others who were aspiring writers. Then too, the editorial desks of the major magazines offered critical advice and blunt evaluations of the writing efforts of well-known businessmen they were trying to encourage. Johnson soon developed a stable of tutors, some of whom surely did not realize what they were getting into.

With journalist friends, like Walter Troan of the *Chicago Tribune*'s Washington bureau, Johnson cast himself in the role of student. He wrote Troan, who was helping him edit a manuscript: "Unfortunately I never write except as a direct result of convictions; therefore, I am usually in trouble. Perhaps there is another aspect of my writing that you may sense, though no one ever tells me about it. I may be too aggressive, controversial, or downright quarrelsome. I suppose it is only natural that some of the heat of my feelings gets into the manuscript."

Johnson believed magazine editors were wary of him because he had strong convictions, but he never quite realized that was actually why they found him appealing. When they would tone down a first draft, Johnson always reacted. "Magazines are afraid of most of my stuff," he wrote a reporter friend. "They seem to have the courage of a sickly gazelle."

"THREE STEPS TO MORAL BUSINESS"

Whenever he wrote an article he felt strongly about but couldn't get published, he resorted to printing it in pamphlet form. The distribution included business associates outside of the company, Johnson & Johnson employees, and others. To his credit, he always submitted his articles, the published ones as well as the non-published, to others for review before they were sent around the company.

One unpublished piece titled, "Three Steps to Moral Business," did not find favor with editors, but it was a thoughtful expression of Johnson's long-held belief that business and morals were intertwined. In it he wrote:

> Three steps must be taken, it seems to me, if moral principles are to guide human relations in the world of business. The first step requires each employer to realize that he is bound by the laws of God to act justly toward his employees and to insure their welfare. It makes no difference whether he derives this obligation from encyclicals of the Pope, from statements by the Federal Council of Churches, or from the Law of Moses–the Torah–with its profound recognition of human rights and duties. The obligation exists, and unless it is accepted nothing else will count.
>
> The second step is for businessmen to adopt an attitude of trusteeship. Today's employer is not the dictator of an economic empire. He is a trustee for investors and customers, for the people of his community, and especially for the men and women who make his business go. He must see that the rights of each group are protected and must make sure that all derive benefit from his policies.

Finally, businessmen must resolve to treat their employees as fellow human beings, not as mere animated machines. Wage earners are men and women; they have rights, dignity, ambition, pride, and they feel a deep need to stand well in the eyes of their associates. Until employers treat them accordingly, business will not act in accord with sound moral principles.

RIDING HERD ON COMPANY ADVERTISING

Johnson also waged war against overstatement in company advertising. "Exaggeration is not good advertising," he insisted. "If you must be off the line, understate rather than overstate." On another occasion he proclaimed: "Should it be that all our firms, worldwide, are the only honest advertisers in the world . . . LET IT BE SO!"

Normally Johnson did not require that all advertising be approved by him, but he did read and evaluate it with great care. It might have been easier if he had prior approval, though, for when he found mistakes the entire campaign had to be abandoned. Repeated mistakes brought out his cutting criticism. Once he spotted an advertisement for a new Red Cross Improved Bandage that embodied all the mistakes he had urged the agency to avoid. His memo to the account executive was devastating:

> When a mistake is made it is unfortunate. When we make the same mistake a second time it is serious. When we make the same mistake a third time we are guilty of incompetence, poor management and lack of competitive strength. When we make the same mistake fifteen or twenty times it is reprehensible.
>
> You will note the attached advertisement. While the signature of Johnson & Johnson is improved it should be appreciably enlarged.
>
> After long and contemplated consideration I conclude that you have generated a group deserving a new terminology. Henceforth such persons will be known as QUARTER-WITS.
>
> ROBERT W. JOHNSON

An outburst like that was not typical. Usually he was more restrained and constructive. He never criticized the agency directly, but always through his own executives. And he did praise advertising he found appealing. Sometimes the praise was generous. But if a memo from him started off like "The Cotton Bud advertising is fairly good . . . ," trouble was sure to follow. "Fairly good" to Johnson meant not as good as the words suggested. His instructions in that particular memo shot a gaping hole in the entire campaign. Suddenly "fairly good" was a disaster.

Johnson didn't rely solely on his own instincts and judgment. Once when he became upset over baby product advertising but couldn't put his finger on the problem, he arranged to bring in a panel of young mothers to discuss the effectiveness of the advertising (the forerunner of focus groups). He had the session tape-recorded so he could listen to their reactions later. Then he outlined what he wanted done in a memo, adding: "I hope this has the consent of Young & Rubicam." It did.

Though Johnson's close attention to company advertising caused some grumbling, there was, over time, unmistakable improvement in all the company's advertising. It did become more dramatic and simpler. While there were jokes about the small white cards printed with his formula for good advertising, years later those cards were still on display in many offices. Most agreed that his formula worked. Johnson would not permit a competitor's product to be mentioned – let alone criticized – in his company's advertising. If a product couldn't be sold on its merits, then it shouldn't be advertised, he maintained.

JOHNSON THE SKILLED MARKETER

As the business grew, so did Johnson & Johnson's reputation for being a skilled marketer of consumer products and an innovator of creative advertising. In the late 1940s an unusual marketing campaign added considerably to this reputation. The advertising of Modess brand sanitary napkins made by the Personal Products

Company had been less than successful, and because of his concern about the product, Johnson often attended the advertising strategy meetings. One day he suggested that the next campaign be pegged to high fashion, a subject of interest to many women. He cautioned, however, that for the campaign to be successful the designer clothes, the models, the settings, and the photographers would all have to be far different from anything ever seen in magazine advertising.

Taking Johnson at his word, the product director and the agency account executives set out to do something radically different with a high-fashion theme. Many of the great couturiers – Valentina, Falkenstein, Hattie Carnegie, Balenciaga, Jacques Fath, Christian Dior – were engaged to design gowns to be used exclusively for the Modess ads. Famous fashion models, including Dorian Leigh and Susie Parker, were photographed by such notables as Ruzzie Green, Cecil Beaton, and Valentino Sarra. The exotic settings ranged from Park Avenue penthouses and European palaces, to Venetian canals, art museums of the world, and the snowcapped mountains of Switzerland.

The "Modess . . . *because*" campaign was an immediate success and was later chosen as one of the hundred all-time great advertisements. Sales of the product soared. But of all its clever aspects, the two simple words of the copy, "Modess . . . *because*" were the most ingenious. That too was actually Johnson's suggestion, according to a marketing executive present the day it was proposed. "When it came to the question of copy," he recalled, "we knew from past experience that women resisted reading about a sanitary napkin, no matter how well written. We were discussing this problem with General Johnson, and he said: 'Think in terms of as few words as possible, perhaps only ten words, maybe only five words, maybe only one word, just "Modess," maybe "Modess . . . *because*."'" The brilliance of the "Modess . . . *because*" copy was that it enabled each woman who read it to fill in her own reasons for wanting to buy the product.

SUPERIOR CONSUMER PRODUCTS

By now many Johnson & Johnson consumer products had become institutions throughout America, and in many other parts of the world as well. Mothers by the millions dusted babies' bottoms with Johnson's Baby Powder and used copious amounts of its sister products – oil, lotion, and baby soap. Johnson's baby products had become synonymous with infant care, and the advertising slogan "Best for Baby – Best for You" lured countless adult users as well. The nostalgic scent of the baby powder was a pleasant reminder of the serene days of childhood, and the formula for the scent was so prized that for decades it was kept in a bank vault.

"First-aid" and the name "Johnson's" had become inseparable in the minds of consumers. Band-Aid adhesive bandages were being used by the billions, and the agency executive who had once predicted they wouldn't sell had retreated into merciful anonymity. Though hospital patients were less aware of the Johnson products used in their care, that was not true of the physicians and nurses who applied the surgical dressings or closed the wounds with Ethicon sutures. They constituted another army of loyal supporters of "The Most Trusted Name in Surgical Dressings."

Like his father, Johnson was relentless in his pursuit of quality and superior products. "We are dedicated to the unwavering determination to design, produce, package and deliver to the ultimate user the finest products in the world," he told his management. "Nothing less offers a reasonable chance of continued success."

In fact, the slightest hint of a drop in quality infuriated him. One senior executive made the mistake of writing Johnson: "There is no instance where our surgical dressings products are not *at least* as good as any competitor's, and in some cases we enjoy a quality advantage." Johnson scrawled in oversize letters on the memo: "NOT GOOD ENOUGH – RWJ" and sent it back.

"A CLUTTERED DESK IS A CLUTTERED MIND"

One of his many passions was neatness in all forms, which was manifested in many ways. Those who worked with him knew he was a confirmed advocate of having a clean desk. Not just his own – he wanted everyone's desk to be clean. So, on his surprise "What's new?" visits he always cast a critical eye on the desktop. Marketing people especially were sometimes barely visible behind the mounds of paper on their desks, including the deluge of memos from Johnson. Numerous times they quoted him as saying: "A cluttered desk is a cluttered mind." In the cafeteria at lunch, or over a beer on the way home, they often talked about the perfect reply: "Yes, General, a cluttered desk is a cluttered mind, and what does an empty desktop suggest to you?" It was good for laughs, but no one ever said it to him.

His penchant for neatness and cleanliness extended to the manufacturing plants, but in this case it was based on his strong conviction that a company producing sterile surgical products had to be clean and properly maintained. "Maintenance is money in the bank," he contended. When it came to plant cleanliness, he was the strongest enforcer, and he did it in strange but effective ways. In the early days, when the factory buildings were old, he ordered all the corners of the factory floor and stairwells painted white so he could easily detect any accumulation of dirt.

Many of the plant inspections were announced in advance. On one the plant manager had a thirty-minute tip prior to his arrival, so he hastily had things spruced up by having several large rolls of paper hoisted to the roof of the building. When Johnson arrived he was furious. "What in the hell is all that junk on the roof?" he asked. He had come by helicopter that day.

JOHNSON WRITES "OR FORFEIT FREEDOM"

Long before the war came to an end the struggle for power in the peacetime economy had begun in workplaces all over America. Labor and management jockeyed to strengthen their positions.

Against this backdrop of national unrest and growing bitterness, Johnson began work on a book that he hoped would address the problems plaguing the nation and offer viable solutions.

Out of this thinking, this concern, came the book *Or Forfeit Freedom: People Must Live and Work Together*, published by Doubleday & Company in 1947. It was the best writing he had ever done, and the *Saturday Review* called it "one of the most important books ever written by an American businessman." Writing the book gave Johnson the opportunity to bring together his philosophy on managing a business, his long-held concerns for the well-being of lower-echelon employees, and his commitment to the community, and to shape all these concepts into a solution to the troubles that business and industry were facing in the turbulent postwar era.

In the opening pages, in his usual blunt style, Johnson summed up his views on the decline of confidence in business:

> Things have been going wrong with our economic system; they went very wrong in 1929 and again in 1937, and they took another tailspin during 1946. Because they did, and because a few business leaders both talked and practiced nonsense, private enterprise is in disgrace with one part of the public and on probation with the rest. . . . Yet the very ones who buy and boast [about products] no longer trust business to do its job well, at a reasonable profit, and with justice for everyone. . . .
>
> This is shown by the number of people who suspect the motives of business, sneer at its claims to service, and favor punitive taxation. It also appears in such studies as the Fortune Survey. During 1946, for example, the Survey revealed an increase of more than forty per cent in the number of people who opposed

business management in its disputes with labor. Though all income groups were represented, the shift was greatest among the middle class and poor, who form most of our population. Can we doubt, then, that business is still losing public confidence?

THE ALL-IMPORTANT PREFACE TO THE CREDO

Throughout the book, Johnson kept his eye on the target: putting America back on the road to full production, full employment, full recognition of labor's rights, and full use of the technical mastery the nation had demonstrated during World War II. Failure to do these things would only encourage further government controls, he wrote, and nothing can be accomplished unless both labor and management redefine their responsibilities to the worker and to society.

Johnson reinforced the point by including in this book a slightly modified version of the "Industrial Credo" that appeared in *"But, General Johnson"* in 1944. This time he added a brief "preface" that gave a compelling rationale for the document and set the stage for his enumeration of a company's social responsibilities. Unfortunately, however, in later years the preface was rarely included with the Credo, as it was meant to be, even though many believed that what it said was vital to the whole concept. The Preface:

> We may be sure that both alarm and bitter anger will arise if huge corporations either abuse their power or fail to render the service required by society. The evidence on this point is clear. American institutions, both public and private, exist because the people want them, believe in them, or at least are willing to tolerate them. The day has passed when business was a private matter – if it ever really was. In a business society, every act of business has social consequences and may arouse public interest. Every time business hires, builds, sells, or buys, it is acting for the American people as well as for itself, and it must be prepared to accept full responsibility for its acts.

The strength of the Credo's message was in its simplicity, and in Johnson's conviction that it was not only a socially responsible approach but also a smart way to run a business. It had been ten years since he first introduced the concept of corporate social responsibility to fellow industrialists. Later he broadened the list of responsibilities to include the communities where employees worked and lived, and make other minor changes, but he never changed the basic concepts.

In many respects, the book was a compendium of Johnson's management philosophy, tuned to the trying times of a nation left badly scarred by a costly war. The message was, in effect, "Let's sit down and talk." It was sensitive to the needs of many, including returning war veterans who came back from hostile battlefields hoping to settle down to a decent-paying job only to find themselves facing a belligerent and divided workplace. It was practical in its approach to solutions – "Five years of good management would do it," Johnson wrote. But it was also idealistic, and that was always Johnson's Achilles' heel.

By all measures, the book was Johnson's most distinguished contribution to change. It came out at a time when he was one of the few American industrialists or perhaps the only one bold enough to face the nation's labor-management unrest and offer solutions – even if they came from "Industry's Rebel," the pragmatic idealist.

Throughout the 271 pages of *Or Forfeit Freedom*, Johnson did not make a single reference to his own company, even though Johnson & Johnson had served as a laboratory for his ideas and solutions since he first assumed a management role thirty years earlier. But in a touching gesture he dedicated the book to "Those men and women who have worked with me through the years" and added: "From them I have learned the lesson that business must and can do its work for the good of humanity."

Robert becomes President of J&J in 1932

In the garden of his home

RWJ built scores of beautiful plants
and modern workplaces

Giving a fiery radio talk

With Frank Farrell

HIS PHILOSOPHY INFLUENCED THE NATION

While words of praise about the book – "courageous," "inspirational," "a stirring trumpet" – continued to come from many quarters, the one group Johnson had hoped to reach, had hoped to stir into action, was his fellow industrialists. Many of them wrote him polite notes about the book and its noble intentions, but when Johnson looked around to see if anyone was following his lead, he found he was alone. To realists, that came as no surprise, for as a writer for the *New York Herald Tribune* later commented, "Johnson set off a firecracker in top industry's face."

The book later received the Franklin D. Roosevelt Memorial Foundation Award from the American Political Science Association as the best book of the year in the field of government and human welfare. The citation read:

> For his approach to the perennial problem of improving labor-management relations; For the promise that his suggestions hold for a more equitable functioning of the private enterprise system; For his recognition of the dignity of the worker and his proposals to re-establish the employee's feeling of craftsmanship; and above all for his enthusiasm and firm conviction that this objective can be accomplished, this award is made.

While *Or Forfeit Freedom* did not become the sudden catalyst for change that Johnson hoped it would, a retrospective look at the later 1940s shows that business during that period underwent transformations that coincided with many of the concepts Johnson was proposing. One shining example was the new relationship that business and industry were developing with the communities where new plants were being built and employees were working as well as living. The bonding between community and business began in the late 1940s and continued to grow. That period also saw a deepening concern on the part of business for the emotional needs of employees in a highly automated work environment – another concept Johnson advanced in his book.

Perhaps most important of all, the message contained in Johnson's Credo influenced similar company statements of responsibility written over the next sixty years. Beginning in 1982, when Johnson & Johnson was confronted by the Tylenol poisonings, the Credo became a landmark document because the company used it as a guide in successfully managing that historic crisis.

RALLYING SUPPORT FOR ETHICS IN BUSINESS

In many of his writings, Johnson came back to several basic themes: human dignity; improving working conditions, from worksite to compensation; blending moral obligations with the pursuit of economic goals; holding business to higher standards of performance in areas where it had not previously ventured. Even before *Or Forfeit Freedom* was published, Johnson had begun to seek ways to gain broader acceptance of these concepts, and he concluded that he would need more support from others. He wrote later: "It seemed to me that I was not qualified to do this task alone. But who was qualified, and how could experts on ethics (which he had decided would be the best place to start) put their ideas into a form that made practical business sense?"

He began by asking a small group of clergymen and businessmen to meet with him in Princeton in the summer of 1946 to help devise a moral code for business. As Johnson spoke to them, the magnitude and complexity of the assignment became apparent to the group, giving rise to doubts that they would be able to accomplish such a formidable task. Yet, Johnson told them, just such a document was needed, not only to bring harmony to the American workplace but also to preserve confidence in the democratic system. "They agreed," he said later, "that no problem [facing the nation] is greater or more urgent than that of establishing sound, cooperative relations between workers and management."

Looking back on the initial meeting, Johnson said: "They reached one unanimous conclusion, that the root of our problem is moral. The human equation is all important. We are dealing with men and women, with all of their hopes and fears, their loves and hates, and not merely with impersonal economic and political forces."

Johnson was skeptical about how the project would develop. "I expected one of two things," he said. "Either the group would develop a useful statement after a few meetings, or there would be polite expressions of interest and the project would die on the vine. Neither of these things happened. To my surprise, all of these experts agreed with my very cautious suggestion that the problem *was* one of ethics. They also went further and declared that giving employment policies a sound ethical basis was the most important issue facing America today. It was also a problem we were determined to solve, regardless of the time or personal sacrifices involved."

LEADERS FROM ALL SECTORS JOIN JOHNSON

No one attending the meeting that day suspected that it would take three years and a score of meetings to complete their work. Shortly after the first meeting, the process of enlarging the group of collaborators began. From the ranks of business they added companies and representatives who had demonstrated a progressive approach to labor-management relations. The labor people who were asked to participate included the widely known and outspoken James B. Carey, Secretary-Treasurer of the Congress of Industrial Organizations (CIO). Boris Shishkin, the economist with the American Federation of Labor (AFL) was another labor representative.

Other Protestant, Jewish, and Catholic clergy were soon added to the group, and the Jesuits were well represented. One prominent Catholic priest was the Rev. John F. Cronin, S.S., an assistant director of the National Catholic Welfare Conference in Washington and a leader of its social-action programs. It was Father Cronin whom the collaborators called on to draft the final document. Several educators were added, including representatives from the Universities of Illinois and Wisconsin, and the Catholic colleges, St. Louis University, Rockhurst, Loyola and Villanova. Rabbi Hirsh E. L. Freund, executive director of the Synagogue Council of America, was one of a number of Jewish leaders who joined the group. The Protestant representation included Dr. Cameron P. Hall, Executive Secretary of the Federal Council of Churches of Christ in America.

As new companies were added, representatives of General Foods Corporation, McCormick & Company Inc., Standard Oil of New Jersey, and Swift & Company joined the group. Two representatives from the Motion Picture Association of America were added, as was Thomas J. Ross of the New York public relations firm of Ivy Lee & T. J. Ross. The meetings were held in various cities every three or four months, including New York, Washington, and Baltimore, and sometimes lasted for two or three days.

HUMAN RELATIONS IN MODERN BUSINESS

The group decided to call the final document "Human Relations in Modern Business: A Guide for Action Sponsored by American Business Leaders," and Prentice-Hall agreed to publish the fifty-two-page document in book format late in 1949. Meanwhile, Johnson, with consent of the group, wrote a major article about the document that appeared in the September 1949 issue of the *Harvard Business Review*. In it he gave the rationale for calling the group together and quoted liberally from the document itself.

The article generated widespread interest in the forthcoming book. Quoting from the document, Johnson wrote: "The world is looking to us for an example of what free men can achieve. We dare not fail. The destiny of generations to come is in our hands – we are making history. This is our challenge, and our opportunity." He also made it clear that it was a cooperative effort, and the names and affiliations of all who participated were listed. The *Harvard Business Review* commented: "The very fact that such a diverse group agreed upon a single document is, in itself, significant."

54

The document began with a Statement of Principles calling attention to the "complex relationship among the various levels of management and labor" and noting: "Men are social creatures, sensitive to considerations of pride, achievement, desire for esteem and affection, and similar non-economic drives. Likewise, men have a conscience and a sense of justice. They do not change their nature when they put on their business suits or working clothes."

These concepts, and the language, were alien to labor management discussions, and certainly to contract negotiations. The document continued along its philosophical course:

"The fundamentals of human nature may not be ignored in human relations. . . . There are [five] drives that profoundly influence conduct: man's sense of *dignity* . . . , the need for the *esteem of others* . . . , the basic *instinct for survival* . . . , the desire for *security* . . . , and *social instincts*, [the natural tendency] to associate with those who share their interests and to develop teamwork in pursuing common undertakings."

Moving from the human equation, it made the transition to religious and moral grounds: "Human relations . . . are subject to moral and religious laws that are reflected in the conscience of mankind and which have been confirmed by the experience of men in all ages. If we accept the brotherhood of man under God, important conclusions follow. Each man has an inner dignity, with basic rights and duties. Life has an over-all purpose. Men must judge their conduct, not merely in terms of personal gain or convenience, but also as right or wrong. Service to society, and to personal interest, become important. Teamwork and cooperation follow."

After giving a historical review of labor and management practices, and abuses, the document offered a perspective on the practical application of the new approaches it was advocating. It discussed basic needs of employees in the workplace environment, personnel policies, employee rights, labor unions and grievances, educational programs, and the need for better communications. Each was elevated to a level that encouraged greater awareness of human needs and a sensitivity to what was considered fair and moral. That was the theme that permeated the entire report, and broke new ground and set the stage for changing future discussions between labor and management.

WIDELY ACCLAIMED AS LANDMARK DOCUMENT

Prentice-Hall printed tens of thousands of the reports and sold them in bookstores and other outlets for $1.50. The committee sent thousands more to industry and labor, business associations, government officials both federal and state, religious leaders, educators, and the press all over the United States. A surge of positive reaction quickly followed publication. The *Harvard Business Review* called it "A Magna Carta for business." *Time* magazine described it as "The Capitalist Manifesto" (the *Communist Manifesto*, by Karl Marx, had been published a century earlier in Germany). The daily and weekly press, labor journals, and religious and education publications all joined in praise of the book.

The overall impact that *Human Relations in Modern Business* had on hastening change during the postwar period is difficult to gauge, because many other factors came into play at the same time. However, the overwhelming national response from various quarters – business, labor, religion, government, and the press – suggests that the principles the document espoused did gain a place on the American agenda in mid-century, for it was during this period that business and industry began to assume a role of greater responsibility. In the workplace the human relations factor became more important, and the rancor that had set in following the war did subside. It was also during this period that business and the community began developing a closer relationship.

The evolution of industrial America in the post-World War II era, from a focus on frenetic production to a pace that had to accommodate the needs of people rather than battlefields, produced no monumental heroes. But a small number of farsighted businessmen who had a sense of what was needed to move the nation forward had emerged. Robert Wood Johnson was one of those leaders, perhaps the most vocal one. Although it was not fully recognized at the time, in retrospect his concepts and philosophy coincided with changes that took place during the period he was advocating them.

Johnson's passionate belief that business organizations had a responsibility to their customers, employees, the community, and stockholders, in that order, began to be viewed as pragmatic rather than altruistic – which Johnson himself had maintained was the case since he first introduced the concept in 1935. Putting the customer first was sound business, not altruism, he said. But it was concern for the employees of the nation – and later the communities where employees worked and lived – that took center stage during a period of turbulence and uncertainty after World War II.

Johnson had been quick to grasp the significance of what was happening in this domestic conflict, and *Human Relations in Modern Business* brought a sense of hope and purpose to the deliberations. It was by all measurements a unique document, and a half-century later it still retains its ring of truth.

JOHNSON FOR SECRETARY OF COMMERCE?

There were recurring rumors in late September 1946 that President Harry S. Truman planned to appoint Johnson as the new Secretary of Commerce, to replace Henry A. Wallace, who had resigned at the President's request. Wallace had been Vice President during Franklin Roosevelt's third term, and Truman had replaced him on the ticket for Roosevelt's fourth term. Although Truman brought Wallace back as Secretary of Commerce, he was a strong-willed opponent of the "get tough" stand the administration had taken against Russia. The breach between the two men soon widened, and Wallace was out.

The *New York Herald-Tribune* gave credence to the rumor with a two-column front-page story quoting White House sources as saying that Johnson was the President's first choice for the Commerce post. Business had been clamoring for a businessman to head the department, and in Johnson the President had a highly visible businessman who had been accepted by both parties. Another candidate mentioned in the story was W. Averell Harriman, then Ambassador to England.

Reporters pressed Johnson for a response, and his reply was emphatic. He was not interested in returning to the bureaucratic wars in Washington, and while he would remain active and vital politically, he did not want to be Secretary of Commerce. Almost immediately Truman offered the position to Harriman, who accepted. Those who knew Johnson's proclivity for saying what was on his mind, and Truman's reputation for giving sharp responses, felt that the decorum at Cabinet meetings would have suffered badly had Johnson been given the appointment.

"DIG, SON, DIG" STIRS CONTROVERSY

As the politics of the Cold War intensified late in 1946, there was increasing concern about the perils of atomic warfare, and rampant speculation about whether the United States, or any nation, could survive a concentrated attack with nuclear weapons. The horror of such a prospect numbed the mind, but military strategists began mapping plans that called for surviving an initial attack while still retaining the ability to strike back. Critical to this strategy would be protection of the nation's defense, and offense, industry. For some time now, Johnson had been pondering how industry might survive a nuclear attack. Late in 1946 he wrote a jolting article titled "Dig, Son, Dig," which touched off a storm of controversy that played out on front pages and radio programs all across the nation. One newspaper headline characterized the article as "a bombshell."

The article appeared the first week of January 1947 in *Army Ordnance*, the journal of the Army Ordnance Association. The goal of the association, comprising 50,000 executives and engineers of American industry, as well as officers of the armed services, was to enhance industrial preparedness for the nation's defense. With thirty-two local chapters spread all over the country, and well-attended national and sectional meetings, it was a powerful organization that carried weight throughout the military-defense establishment. Johnson was a frequent contributor to the journal.

Like many of Johnson's ideas, this one had a fuse ready to be lighted. In the article, Johnson called for industry and government to collaborate on a plan to protect industry from atomic attack and suggested underground plants as one possibility. The spark was provided by the catchy "Dig, Son, Dig" headline in the usually staid journal. When translated to newspaper headlines, Johnson's proposal for a defense plan quickly became a frantic plea to start digging. The *New York Times*, the *Herald-Tribune*, the *Washington Post*, and the *Baltimore Sun* ran the story on page one. Waves of editorial opinion followed, as the "Ban the Bomb" adherents, the doves, and the hawks entered the fray. Ministers felt compelled to speak out, one calling Johnson's suggestion "morally repugnant."

It was a moot point for, from any angle, the article was not about to calm fears. "The atomic bomb is a reality," he wrote. "It may soon be possible to destroy the power of an industrialized nation in a few days, or even a few hours. If we have a third world war, that is what the enemy will attempt to do to us – destroy us in the first days of war. In the past two wars, our production lines were the fountainheads of victory. In a third war, an enemy could have no choice but to attempt to choke off the flow of these fountainheads at once. If the enemy should have its way, the Arsenal of Democracy would become the prime theater of war."

Johnson went on to recommend that this was a decision that neither the military nor the government should make independently. "This job calls for civilian leadership, not Civil Service – God forbid!" he wrote. "We in business are ready to develop a defense. . . . We are determined that this time the defense will not be fouled up by official red tape."

Then religious leaders expressed opposition to underground plants, saying that this approach would weaken their efforts to emphasize moral barriers to atomic warfare. Actually, the Army-Navy Munitions Board had already appointed an Underground Site Committee and authorized it to survey potential locations. Johnson's article mentioned the possibility of building plants in caves and caverns, and Richard R. Deupree, Chairman of the Munitions Board and CEO of Procter & Gamble, told the *New York Times* that Johnson's article prompted a flood of calls from cave and cavern owners who thought they had found a new market for their properties. (The *Times* speculated that stalactites and stalagmites would be a problem.)

AN EXCHANGE WITH TRUMAN AND EISENHOWER

The threat of nuclear war would continue to be a constant concern that would hover over the nation for many years. Johnson's article stirred the debate about how to deal with the threat, and the press brought to light several previously undisclosed attempts to explore moving defenses underground – not just manufacturing, but military, government, and staff personnel as well. Several weeks after publication of his article, Johnson wrote to both Truman and Dwight D. Eisenhower, then Chief of Staff in the War Department. The letters were prompted by a new British report on the devastation of atomic bombing, and his question to both men was: "What can we do in the United States to strengthen our defense against this type of weapon?"

Truman chose to inject politics into his reply: "I wish everyone in the United States could have seen not only Hiroshima and Nagasaki but Berlin, London and a dozen other places that I can name. I think then we would never go isolationist again. Some of the Republicans seem headed in that direction and we must stop it if we can."

General Eisenhower's reply to Johnson, addressing him as "Mr. Johnson," not "General," noted that a jointly sponsored analysis by the British and Americans of bombing damage in Europe and Japan was expected to produce guidelines for building better defenses for the Allies. "I truly appreciate your patriotic interest in this subject," he added.

People often mentioned Johnson's deep sense of patriotism. He wrote and spoke about preserving freedom in America, and about allegiance to flag and country, with passion and visible emotion that could bring tears to his eyes. "The banner of freedom is as fresh and new today as it was when the rugged pioneers came to America," he wrote. "The crusading challenge of Valley Forge has been lost in the shuffle of foreign ideologies, but the truth is as real as it was to the soldiers under Washington. Our parents gave us the heritage of independence. Are we throwing it away? Freedom is still the brightest, shiniest, newest, most radical thought in the world."

Claiming that business held the key to tarnishing the appeal of communism, Johnson said: "The new purpose of business is to do everything so well that socialism and communism will cease to exist. It is no longer enough to produce a better product at a lower price. Business is our way of life and must accept the responsibility for all of the economic effects of our capitalistic system. . . . The handwriting is clear. American institutions, whatever their nature, exist through public sufferance. The new purpose of business is to serve the public, both with products and a code of ethics. We must perform all of the services that the public demands. If we do not, the voters will choose another system. . . . Once the public has made up its mind that our present system is inadequate, it will be too late to either repair it or defend it. . . . The new purpose of business is not only to do these things but to explain them to the people."

BRINGING COLLEGE TO THE WORKPLACE

For someone who was constantly churning out new ideas, he had many more successes than failures. And then there were the good ideas that never got off the ground because they proved to be impractical. One such project was his idea for turning factories into places of learning, a concept he called "College While You Work." As always, he approached a new project with boundless enthusiasm and was miffed when others did not respond in a like manner. His plan was to offer college courses to production and office workers at the worksite, and mostly on company time.

"Workers cannot live happily or well in a world they do not understand," he wrote in his outline for the project, which he hoped would result in "a student body of 30 million." Using adult-education and plant-training courses as models, Johnson wanted to expand to include college-level courses in three areas: job-related courses like accounting and engineering; courses dealing with problems related to the family, labor relations, and international affairs; and cultural courses, which he described as ranging from "English to Egyptology." Some would extend beyond the work day into the evenings, but the "campus" would still be the company facility.

As someone who had not attended college, Johnson had a particular concern for others who hadn't, and here he thought he had a solution to a better education. "Why not do it at the place of work," he said, "and why not as a business expense? True, such a plan would call for additional overhead, but if it pays off in terms of lower costs then the scheme would not be an expense but a profit."

He added: "Were every business and every employer to undertake his own educational program in collaboration with their employees, and carried out in cooperation with unions, we would carry education throughout our working years. To think and think straight requires an ever-lasting flow of new facts. Unless we are prepared to expose our job holders to these new factors, how can we hope that they will understand the complexities of our age?"

It was a compelling argument, especially for employees. Least enthusiastic were the manufacturing people, who believed "College While You Work" would play havoc with their production schedules. For months Johnson tried to sell the idea to his fellow industrialists, who listened to his plan with polite indifference. He had paid several educators to work out a sample curriculum – and with that as a basis for an article, he tried to interest the *Saturday Evening Post*. They listened, but weren't buying. At his own company he could generate no enthusiasm whatsoever. No one thought it would work. Finally, the idea began to fade away. Johnson remained its only champion.

"A DAY IN MODERN INDUSTRY" FOR YOUTH

But for every Johnson idea that was abandoned, many more flourished. One that proved very successful was "A Day in Modern Industry," targeted at high school students about to graduate. In planning the project, Johnson remarked: "If industries would let the nation's youth be a part of industry for one day, millions of our citizens of tomorrow would have a new concept of the vital role that management plays in making possible our high standard of living." Months were spent planning the program and making a film to be used in schools and to encourage other companies to invite high school seniors to spend a day in industry, where they could "manage the company" for a day by assuming duties of key positions.

Not one to coddle young people, or anyone else, Johnson had some very direct words for the first of many high school groups that came to the company as part of the program. "American youth lacks the initiative of our pioneers," he told them, "and adults are to blame because you prefer personal security to pioneering. This is our attempt to show young men and women about to be on their own the roles that imagination and initiative have played in building American industry. Youth must be shown their responsibilities and sold on the American way of life. Our important duty of the day is to give you the facts and the truth."

That first day, three hundred students participated in the program, and a seventeen-year-old from St. Peter's High School sat at Johnson's desk and became "chairman of the board." The news media turned out in force, with fifteen national publications, wire services, and radio networks represented. In later years, with the help of continued press interest and promotion by Johnson's personnel department, "A Day in Modern Industry" was widely replicated by other companies.

UNCOMPROMISING ON THE CREDO

Though strong-willed and highly opinionated, Johnson nonetheless tolerated discussion and debate on many business matters. He had an excellent management group, and he always claimed that he was wise enough to listen to them. In one area of the business, however, he was adamant, and that was in adhering strictly to the principles laid down in the Johnson & Johnson Credo. The Credo was law, and as long as he was running the company it would be followed to the letter. Anyone who didn't comply could look for another job. He made that point unmistakably clear.

Though an idealist in many respects, Johnson was also a pragmatic, hardheaded businessman, and he applied this sense of reality to the Credo. "This Credo is not perfect," he wrote. "We have changed it and expect to change it again. We also know that it is better than we are; being humanly frail we sometimes find it difficult to live up to its declarations. But we believe that it is both a set of goals and a guide which helps us to do better than we would without it."

HAILED AS "AN AMERICAN BUSINESS LEADER"

By the late 1940s Johnson had become one of the nation's most articulate and forward-thinking business leaders. His reputation was constantly being reinforced by a steady string of feature stories about him in national magazines and newspapers. He drew from a wellspring of new ideas, and his interviews were sprinkled with the kind of colorful quotes that delighted journalists.

He had a knack for putting together just the right mix of words to create a punchy, often shocking, and sometimes even amusing phrase to enliven a story. "Every time I hear the term 'common labor,' it hits me in the belly." Or, on decentralization: "Put a man in charge, give him elbow room, and go fishing." Or, on where to locate a factory: "Place the plant where it best belongs, and not in a place just because the old man who founded the business was born there."

This Week magazine, the nationally syndicated newspaper supplement, referred to him in a headline as "America's Most Unorthodox Big Businessman" in the January 4, 1948, edition of the Sunday *New York Herald-Tribune*. Journalist Jack H. Pollack was quickly caught in the Johnson web: "A slender, dapper boyish 54, Johnson is a complex personality. Though he laughs easily, relaxes with his feet on the desk and barks orders like a typical tycoon, he is essentially serious, sensitive and introverted. Author of the controversial book *Or Forfeit Freedom*, he is a constant headache to more conservative fellow industrialists."

Johnson always managed to work into the interview some of his favorite solutions. That day he addressed the welfare problem: "The eleven million people earning less than a subsistence living are a liability to society, which must meet the deficit to feed them and their families through charity and subsidies. Why not avoid this waste and pay the bill at its source with a living wage?"

The writer exuded abundant praise over the design of Johnson's factories: "Every day, on much-traveled U.S. Route 1 between New York and Philadelphia, motorists blink their billboard weary eyes in disbelief. For rising out of these grimy smokestack surroundings is a white-marbled, green landscaped building which looks like a Hollywood version of the Twenty-First Century. No mirage. It is Robert Johnson's 'Factory of the Future.' . . . The Employees have their own showers, modern cafeterias, lounges, where they play bridge and ping-pong – and a plant broadcasting system for dances and educational programs."

DESCRIBED AS "THIRTY YEARS AHEAD OF HIS TIME"

In a rare moment, exhibiting doubt about whether some of his concepts would ever be accepted, Johnson said a better time for new ideas would be coming – when the nation wasn't enjoying so much prosperity – for in a downturn people are more apt to listen to new ideas. But then he quickly reverted to the Johnson everyone knew: "I am not worried about the future of my company, but about the future of American industry."

Newsweek magazine called him the "Lone Wolf" of American business, saying that he "was born with a silver spoon in his mouth, but has replaced it with a gold one." The steady growth and success of Johnson's family of companies was compelling evidence that, despite his maverick tendencies, he knew how to build a business. The magazine noted the recent flurry of plant expansion, presided over by Johnson and "exemplifying Johnson's belief that factories can be beautiful as well as useful."

Of one of the new factories, *Modern Industry* magazine said:

> It might be an H. G. Wells industrial futurama . . ., production workers in spotless blue and white uniforms . . ., foremen in surgeons' coats. Lustrous aluminum paint. Restful light-colored walls and dirt-free buff floors. Machinery completely enclosed to keep dirt out. Neatness, efficiency. To effect a workable compromise between his dream machines (with all parts enclosed), Johnson employed a sculptor who has made a hobby of streamlining industrial equipment. The sculptor is now busy designing panels to cover ready-made machinery. . . .
>
> What kind of person is this highpowered, scrupulous industrial manager whose main difficulty is being thirty years ahead of his time? His management ideas are sound, they say, but sometimes get so far ahead of the main stream that carrying them out creates practical problems.

When *Cosmopolitan* magazine asked how young people could get ahead in business, Johnson advised: "If the boss doesn't think you're good, quit the job."

A group of young business executives searching for more youthful views on business management decided to form the Young Presidents Organization. They asked Johnson, then fifty-seven, to speak at their first dinner meeting. Despite the age difference, the group believed that Johnson represented a new generation of management-thinking. In a rousing talk, he urged them to go out and regain the confidence the public had lost in business twenty years earlier. "Business must get back the respect of the man on the street if it hopes to remove itself as a sitting duck for driveling politicians to shoot at," he told them.

NAMED AN HONORARY FELLOW OF
THE AMERICAN COLLEGE OF SURGEONS

Many awards and honors for his contributions to and interest in medicine came Johnson's way, but none moved him as much as becoming the first layman to be named an Honorary Fellow of the American College of Surgeons. In accepting the award at the College's annual convocation in Boston in the fall of 1950, Johnson was moved. "This fulfills the ambition of a lifetime. Now I am almost a doctor," he told the gathered surgeons. Frequently he referred to the award as "one of the highlights of my life." The same honor was later bestowed on him by the Royal College of Surgeons in England, when he was made a member of the Court of Patrons of that august group.

At times Johnson had reflected career paths he might have taken, and becoming a physician was always high on his list. Over time he acquired a remarkable amount of knowledge on medical subjects, sometimes to the amazement of doctors who either treated him or were collaborating on a medical project. It was his usual practice to read everything he could find on a particular medical subject and to consult the experts in that field. In analyzing the state of his own health, he frequently got too many expert opinions, prompting one physician to write him: "Wealthy people who have access to too many experts, and the wives of physicians, are, for different reasons, among those who are poorest cared for."

He became deeply involved in the restructuring of Middlesex Hospital and for six years served as chairman of its executive committee. He encouraged company executives to volunteer their time too, and there was a steady succession of them among the hospital's volunteer leadership. Johnson always had a deep personal interest in how hospitals were managed, and as with business he felt it could always be done better. It was not unusual for him to visit the hospital several days a week, roaming the corridors with several "recruits" from Johnson & Johnson in tow – time and motion study experts, engineers, accountants, personnel specialists – any discipline that could contribute to improvement.

He soon expanded this project to include numerous other hospitals in the area, and he persuaded the area chapter of the Society for the Advancement of Management to send new volunteers. In time, his efforts gained national attention, and the *Reader's Digest* published an article about the reforms Johnson was helping to bring about in hospitals and the volunteer movement spreading across the nation, which they gave him credit for.

JOHNSON'S CAMPAIGN ON BEHALF OF NURSES

Nursing was another area of patient care close to Johnson's heart. Well-trained nurses, he believed, should have a more important role and could be given greater responsibility for patient care. He did not hesitate to say that physicians were part of the problem because a subservient role had been carved out for nurses. Several programs to elevate the professional status of nurses were sponsored by Johnson, and as far away as Brazil he funded a nursing program, which was named for him. He also devised a program to bring nurses out of retirement to meet a current shortage.

Years later, his interest in nursing inspired the founding of the Johnson & Johnson Wharton School Fellows Program in Management for Nurse Executives at the University of Pennsylvania, the leading program of its kind in the nation. But the innovative nursing program at the Wharton School was only one of Johnson's many legacies. In recognition of his personal commitment to Middlesex Hospital and his generous financial gifts, the hospital was later renamed the Robert Wood Johnson University Medical Center and became one of the premier hospitals in New Jersey. The medical school at Rutgers University became the Robert Wood Johnson Medical School. But the primary legacy was The Robert Wood Johnson Foundation in Princeton, New Jersey, the nation's largest philanthropy devoted to improving health care.

ROBERT JOHNSON: "MAN ABOUT TOWN"

Johnson had mentioned to his journalist friend Frank Farrell the possibility of coming to work for him, but Farrell resisted. He explained why: "I admired and respected [Johnson], and truly liked him, but it doesn't surprise me that people didn't get close to him. When I was a kid I trained polo ponies for General George Patton. I was one of Patton's favorite characters. But as I studied Patton, I swore to myself it's a good thing we're friends and I don't have to work for him, because I would go crazy. And I swore that I would never get into the Army because he might request me and I couldn't work for him. He tried to get me to go to West Point, and I'll tell you that's one of the reasons I volunteered for the Marine Corps (during World War II, Farrell was a captain in the Office of Strategic Services and served in the South Pacific), to stay away from Patton. My relationship with Bob Johnson is the same. As long as we were on a parallel as personalities where wealth didn't matter, fine. But the idea of working for Bob, no. I never gave it a moment's thought."

Farrell, a handsome, charismatic columnist for the *New York World-Telegraph and Sun,* covered nightlife in Manhattan and also wrote about more serious subjects. His engaging Irish manner, quick wit, and ready smile made him enormously popular with the ladies. Being single, he was a popular choice of the Hollywood studios to escort their rising young starlets around New York, making the rounds of Copacobana, the Stork Club, El Morocco, "21" and others in that glittering orbit – naturally becoming "items" in the next day's columns. Farrell escorted Elizabeth Taylor when she was a rising star, and later he was linked romantically to a string of starlets, including Rhonda Fleming and Maureen O'Hara. He loved New York and knew it well, later being largely responsible for bringing the aircraft carrier *Intrepid* to its Hudson River mooring to become a museum popular with tourists.

Johnson and Farrell forged a friendship that continued for twenty-five years. "I admired Bob Johnson so much," Farrell recalled. "I found him fascinating. To me he was a personal hero; I loved to be with him. He was a very handsome man with a very commanding personality. He had the heartiest laugh, and when he laughed the whole room would turn around, because it was a deep voice and a very honest laugh. He had the voice of a military commander in the field – though not in combat, because combat overturns the voice."

VISITING THE KENNEDYS AT HYANNISPORT

"We did a lot of sailing together on *Gerda* when she was docked at City Island in New York," Farrell said. "We had a Danish captain, a mate and a cook, and Bob and I took turns at the helm and stood regular watches. One time he decided to stop by and see his old friend, Joe Kennedy, at Hyannisport. Jack was there. Bobby was there. Most of the family was there. About five o'clock Joe, Bob, and I were in the library, and Joe said: 'Bob, what about your stock?' Bob replied: 'Joe, it should be selling at about half of what it's selling right now.' Two years later I ran into Joe Kennedy on Fifth Avenue and he said: 'Frank, you must be a millionaire now.' I said, 'No, still working for about $20,000 a year at the newspaper.' He said 'What did you do about Johnson & Johnson stock after I set Bob up for you that day?' I said 'Nothing. I took

Bob at his word. The stock was high.' He said: 'You fool, the chairman of the board can't tip you on his stock. That was the surest statement I've ever heard to buy the stock, because I bought it and made $2 million.' I said, 'Joe, that's how millionaires are made and I guess I'm destined to be a poor man all my life.' He said: 'Frank, keep your ears open on these things.'"

GINGER ROGERS SAYS HE IS A GREAT DANCER

On occasions when his wife was not in town and Johnson was staying at their apartment at the Hotel Pierre, he would join Farrell on his rounds of the cabarets, once with Joan Crawford and several times with Ginger Rogers. "Ginger Rogers called me and Bob the best non-professional dancers in the world, and the papers picked it up," Farrell said. "Johnson was fascinated by Walter Winchell, who was probably one of the extraordinary characters of all time. If he joined Bob and his wife at their table, he would tell them stories for an hour. He loved to tell stories. Bob was never a playboy. He was far superior to those characters. He could belt a few, and then not drink for a week. Now and then he would have a moment of eccentricity."

DEBATING HIS FRIEND BISHOP FULTON SHEEN

"I would love to hear Bob and Fulton Sheen go at it," Farrell recalled. These meetings with the Catholic bishop were usually over lunch or dinner in one of Manhattan's better restaurants, he added. Fulton Sheen (Fulton was his mother's maiden name) had become the best-known Catholic orator in America because of his spellbinding sermons on his weekly network telecast, "Life Is Worth Living," which ran on NBC. He would appear on the set of a study wearing a cape and pectoral cross and in a deep, rich voice make a flawless, forceful presentation without benefit of notes or teleprompter. Set in prime time against Milton Berle and Frank Sinatra, the series was expected to die a quick death, but Fulton Sheen's appeal sent the ratings soaring. Earlier he had hosted "The Catholic Hour" on radio and spent sixteen years in mission work as national director of the Society for the Propagation of the Faith. But it was his television program that

71

catapulted him into national prominence and gave him an entrée to business, society, and politics.

Getting into a discussion with Fulton Sheen on a serious issue was a mental and verbal challenge that intrigued Johnson. A brilliant scholar, the bishop had written more than a score of books, but he was skillful at putting people at ease. He used his humor to great advantage. When he received an Emmy for his television show, he quipped: "I feel it is time I pay tribute to my four writers, Matthew, Mark, Luke, and John." After returning to his television show following a summer-long absence, his opening line was "Long time, no Sheen."

Johnson had great respect for him and did not back off during their many friendly but intense encounters. Farrell recalled the lively discussions between Johnson and Fulton Sheen: "I would hold back and not even enter the conversation unless I thought there was a point they were missing."

"HE FIT DEFINITION OF A GENTLEMAN"

The Bishop too remembered: "We had many discussions. [Johnson's] favorite subject was business, and we were often on opposite sides. He was constantly emphasizing labor-management relationships, and along with that the independence of business from government bureaucracy. The position I took was that business should work toward profit-sharing – that is to say, the workers should be given some share of the profits. In those days there were many sit-down strikes, which had started in France. The argument I gave was that workers were willing to sit down on someone else's tools but not willing to sit down on their own. His position was never that of paternalism, of being good to them just to win their goodwill. His argument was that business required that they be given more than an adequate wage. He often told me that he raised wages above the comparable wage scale of other industries simply because he felt that it was good business. Hence, the response he received, he felt, was as good or better than that which would be received from profit-sharing. . . . I admired him so much."

Sheen also said Johnson fit the definition of a gentleman that John Henry Cardinal Newman gave in his book *The Idea of a University*: "It is almost a definition of a gentleman to say he is one who never inflicts pain." The bishop continued: "We in America are not always inclined to stress decorum and the qualities that go to make a man of refinement. But [Johnson] stood out among other men in that respect, and, as such, I will always remember him."

MOVING INTO PHARMACEUTICALS

In the late 1950s, the senior management decided that in order to keep pace with developments in health care it would be necessary for Johnson & Johnson to expand into pharmaceuticals. The General offered strong resistance. He had created within the company a corporate culture that came as close to being a reflection of one man's thinking as any American business, and the thought of diluting that culture by absorbing another company was abhorrent to him. Further, he had an admonition that had a chilling effect on any negotiations for an acquisition – "Never acquire a business when you can't fire the board of directors or the president."

Finally Johnson relented and said he would go along with acquiring a pharmaceutical company if, in his words, it would be a "right fit." In 1959 the search ended with the acquisition of McNeil Laboratories Inc., which traced its beginnings to a family-owned drugstore in the mill district of Philadelphia in 1879. It later grew into a successful company that was run by Robert L. McNeil and his two sons, Henry and Robert. McNeil specialized in sedation and muscle-relaxant drugs, and later introduced Tylenol, first a prescription product and later an over-the-counter pain remedy that became hugely successful. Johnson liked the "fit," especially the company's heritage and family ownership.

Shortly after, the company learned of the brilliant pharmacological research of a young Belgian physician, Paul Janssen. Borrowing $1,000 from his physician father, Dr. Janssen had opened a small laboratory, with two assistants, in the town of Beerse, Belgium. Over the course of several years, he discovered two original compounds that became successful pharmaceutical products. From this emerged Janssen Pharmaceutica, still very small and highly skilled in research but lacking marketing prowess. That was Johnson & Johnson's strength, and Janssen Pharmaceutica became part of the family of companies. Paul Janssen went on to become one of the world's most prolific and highly acclaimed pharmacological researchers. Over time, he developed more than seventy compounds that became products, five of which were on the World Health Organization's list of "essential drugs."

For Johnson, the acquisition of McNeil was like bringing new relatives into the family. He dealt with that more easily than he did with parting with 622,000 shares of Johnson & Johnson stock, which was what the $31 million acquisition price amounted to. Parting with company stock was always painful for him. Over time, Johnson developed a degree of rapport with the McNeils, especially with Henry, the son, but for years he continued to grumble about the price that was paid for the company. Over the long term it became an excellent investment, but Johnson saw only the shares the company had to part with.

JOHNSON AND PAUL JANSSEN: THE SPARKS FLEW

Janssen, the distinguished scientist, and Johnson, the maverick businessman, were both complex individuals, incurably inquisitive and frequently stubborn. "He liked people who spoke their minds," Dr. Janssen recalled. "I gathered that most people were afraid of him. I was not. On many occasions we had differences of opinion. There were lots of arguments. He wouldn't yield and I wouldn't yield."

The two remained friends and enjoyed each other's company, even when the discussions became heated. In the area of research, though, Dr. Janssen's patience was often tested. "The General had this idea of cottage research," Dr. Janssen recalled, "and that was to hire all these bright people and then build a cottage for them in the middle of the woods somewhere and let them do whatever they wanted. Then they would come out years later with grandiose ideas. I pointed out to him that research was teamwork, certainly in the modern world."

"He was interested in so many things," Dr. Janssen added. "And he was a complicated man. I've never met anyone like him. He's not comparable to anyone I've ever met in my life."

While Johnson had strongly held views on many areas of business, he was wise enough to step aside for progress. His early resistance to building a pharmaceutical business soon changed as the Janssen team began registering success after success. In the years that followed, pharmaceuticals would become the fastest-growing segment of the business.

THE JOHNSON PAVILION AT
THE UNIVERSITY OF PENNSYLVANIA

Over a period of years, Johnson had developed a close relationship with several physicians at the University of Pennsylvania Hospital. One who treated his medical problems was Dr. Francis Wood, an erudite physician who loved literature almost as much as he loved medicine – and who became a good friend of Johnson. Another was Dr. Isador Ravdin, a noted surgeon and cancer specialist who taught generations of medical students at Penn. Ravdin was one of four surgeons who were roused in the middle of the night in 1956 to perform emergency surgery on President Dwight Eisenhower. Whenever Johnson and Ravdin were together they began their playful needling of each other. At one luncheon when Johnson was there to make a major gift, he kidded Dr. Ravdin about "having his hand in my pocket." Ravdin didn't deny it.

Because of the General's relationship with Penn, the Johnson & Johnson Board of Directors decided to give $1.5 million to the university's medical school for a building to be named for him. The six-story teaching, research, and library

75

building would be called The Robert Wood Johnson Pavilion and was to be built along Hamilton Walk, on the main campus in Philadelphia. Johnson approved a brief list of mementos to be placed in the cornerstone – including one of his books and a copy of the Credo – and joined Penn President Dr. Gaylord Harnwell for the cornerstone-laying ceremony. It was a warm summer day, and the podium and chairs for several dozen faculty members and guests were set up on the lawn. Johnson listened to the introductory speeches and then went to the podium to give his response. Just then a group of coeds passed by, and he began his remarks by noting: "My, what a wonderful spot this is for girl-watching."

"I HAVE MADE MANY ERRORS –
BUT NEVER WITH J&J STOCK"

For the most part, Johnson kept an open mind and could be persuaded to revise some of his business decisions of the past, providing the new circumstances warranted it. Decisions could be amended, but he was adamant about holding to his philosophy. One area of decision-making that he considered sacrosanct had to do with matters dealing with the company's stock. "I have made many errors," he said, "but never with Johnson & Johnson stock."

He strongly resisted splitting the stock, even when it was selling at more than $100 a share and had one of the highest multiples (earnings per share) in the health-care industry in the mid-1960s. "Broadly speaking, the market will take care of itself. It is not our desire to run with the pack. Our value in the marketplace will be determined by our competence," he told his management. The argument that a high price per share kept the stock from having broader ownership carried no weight with him, because he preferred having fewer shareholders to begin with – except for his employees. He wanted as many employees as possible to own Johnson & Johnson stock. Not just as a reward, but as an incentive to do their jobs better.

The General could be tough on non-performers. Once he wrote to directors in his companies around the world: "Now is the time to rid ourselves of all weak men and women in management. We have carried borderline cases for many years in the hope that we could improve them and out of a sense of charity. Today, anyone from Johnson & Johnson can find employment. Now is the time to separate them from our team."

"He was a tough taskmaster," a longtime colleague said of Johnson. "He could be difficult and demanding, but he was fair. You could dig yourself into a hole, and that was all right, as long as you could climb out. But when he saw that you couldn't, that was it. The project or the person was finished. He would give you enough rope to hang yourself, and some did."

NO ESCAPING THE GENERAL'S MEMOS

The General's memos demanded attention, but they weren't always easy to deal with. Some of his ideas were farfetched and required more delicate handling. None of his memos died a natural death, because of his efficient system for reviving them from his bulging follow-up file. It wasn't possible, or prudent, to simply ignore a subject he had written about – it demanded either action or a plausible explanation. No subject was ever just forgotten.

For years he followed the practice of having stand-alone cards printed with a motto or message, most of which originated with him. The cards were usually four by six inches and nicely printed on heavy stock with red or gold beveled edging. He would have them distributed to some one hundred executives in the company, usually the same ones who received books from him. Among his favorites were:

MANAGEMENT IS CAUSE
ALL ELSE EFFECT

ANY FOOL CAN SPEND MONEY.
ONLY A COMPETENT MAN CAN
MAKE SOUND AND SECURE PROFITS

THIS IS NO TIME FOR AVOIDANCE
EVASION OR EXCUSES

WHY BE DIFFICULT
WHEN WITH A LITTLE EFFORT
YOU CAN BE IMPOSSIBLE

WE LEARN THE HARD WAY
THAT PROCRASTINATION DEVELOPS
A NEW COMPETITOR

CHANGING OF THE GUARD

Nearly two years had passed since Philip Hofmann succeeded Johnson as Chairman of the Executive Committee in the spring of 1961. Hofmann continued to demonstrate strong leadership, and Johnson seemed quite comfortable with his own reduced role in the company. No one anticipated the decision Johnson was about to make. Late in May 1963, Hofmann was attending a pharmaceutical industry meeting at the Greenbrier, a splendorous resort nestled on the eastern slopes of the Allegheny Mountains in White Sulphur Springs, West Virginia. As the conference was about to end, Hofmann received a call from Johnson, who said he wanted to come down to the Greenbrier to meet with him on a very important matter. The business he wanted to discuss, the General said, would take a few days, and he told Hofmann to reserve one of the resort's cottages, where they would have complete privacy.

Some years later, in a fortuitous encounter aboard the liner *Queen Elizabeth II* on a transatlantic crossing to England, Hofmann related to this author, in leisurely fashion, what took place at the meeting with Johnson at the Greenbrier:

"The General arrived the next morning, and I still had no idea what was on his mind," Hofmann said. "He came right to the point and said he was going to make me Chairman of the Board and Chief Executive Officer of Johnson & Johnson. It came as a complete surprise. No one had been willing to believe that the General was going to step down, because the company was his whole life. Many thought he would never let go.

REVIEW OF COMPANY'S STRENGTHS AND WEAKNESSES

"Over the next three days, he led me through an intensive review of our worldwide operations, company by company. We covered several dozen of our major operations, and for each one we discussed the state of the business, past failures, and future opportunities. And we discussed the strengths and weaknesses of every member of senior management. He had given this very careful thought and planning, and it was extremely well organized. He didn't miss anything.

"During those several days he was reviewing the results of his entire career. He was a great businessman – but a shy man, in many respects – and he had a mind that he couldn't shut off. It was always working. His number-one love was the business, but it wasn't a monetary thing. It was his desire to create a business that would bring better health, serve the welfare of the people, and at the same time make a profit.

"He didn't give me any specific instructions on what I should do as Chairman. He wanted to put the business in the hands of people he trusted, and he was smart enough to know that the most dangerous thing you can do is to write an exact blueprint for an unknown future. He told me he had made mistakes and if I wanted to see them just go to the Kilmer Museum and look at the products that never made it. He chased a lot of rainbows, but he also caught a lot of them. He devoted his life to Johnson & Johnson, and everything else came second.

"But he could be very tough and dogmatic," Hofmann continued. "He was generous to a fault, and he could do very kind things for people. I remember once during the war we were walking up the concourse of the 30th Street train station in Philadelphia, and he was in his brigadier general's uniform. Ahead of us was this little girl in a WAC uniform, and she was struggling with a heavy duffel bag. He came up to her and said, 'Come on, soldier, I'll give you a hand.' He swung the duffel on his shoulder and carried it to the taxi stand. She was all aflutter, having a General carry her duffel.

"He explained to me why he would not be attending any more stockholder meetings. He said someone would be bound to ask what he thought on a subject, and when that happened I would no longer be the Chairman. 'You might have the title,' he said, 'but you wouldn't be the Chairman.' On the second or third day, he asked me to go over the changes I would like to make in the company. I had given it some thought, so I had a list of things I wanted to do, including some extra stock to senior managers that came from me, not from him. He said, 'Fine. Go ahead.'

"From that day forth he never once ordered me to do something his way, and never countermanded a decision I made. I respected him greatly for that, because I know how tough it was for him to let go. This was tested very soon. He came into my office a little later, very enthused about an idea he wanted the company to pursue. It did not appeal to me, and I told him so. He said to me: 'There are two ways to make a decision – one is logic and the other is intuition. If something tells you it's wrong, then forget it.' And we forgot his idea."

The General decided that he would remain on the Board of Directors (later he became chairman of the Finance Committee). Before leaving the Greenbrier, the two agreed on several other key management changes. Gustav O. Lienhard would succeed Hofmann as Chairman of the Executive Committee, and Bobby Johnson (the General's son) and Richard B. Sellars would become chairmen of the Executive Committee.

The Board of Directors that Hofmann headed was made up of twenty-three members of management with a collective total of 581 years of service with the company, or an average of twenty-five years each. They knew one another, and the company, well. They were there because they measured up to the standards of performance that Johnson had set for them, and because each one was personally committed to fulfilling the responsibilities contained in the Credo.

There were no farewell speeches from Johnson, and no messages to employees – no doubt a reflection of his belief that he would still be around tending to things, and in his own way. He did write a memo to the Executive Committee, which began: "It has been my painful duty to review the errors of my chairmanship." He then proceeded to list them, referring mostly to areas of the business that had been hurt by slow decision-making. "We intend to avoid such practice in the future," he said. "Management that is ponderous, slow-thinking, and slow-moving will not survive." It was as much a warning as a confession of his errors.

He was not amused when he tried to call a meeting and found that none of his senior executives was around. That prompted him to write: "Typical of my first week after having shed my important position, I find that everyone is in Europe." On another occasion, he wrote: "I will not be as active, and this will probably be a relief to you [Hofmann], and a good thing for everyone."

Some things did not change, nor could they as long as Johnson was around. A few days after stepping down, he was driving along the highway and came across a group of strikers in front of one of his plants. He stopped and asked if they would move their cars to the rear so they wouldn't detract from the appearance of the building from the highway. He also told them that if it rained he would see to it that management provided a place under cover for them to picket, and that if they were still on strike when winter came he would put up a tent for them. The strikers were delighted to meet "the General," and they chatted with him amiably.

Johnson continued to carve out for himself an area of responsibility that he labeled "forward planning." For years, there had been rampant speculation about what would happen to Johnson & Johnson when he stepped down, but the change brought none of the dire consequences many had predicted. Johnson did not need a title to make his presence felt, or permission to explore those areas of the business that interested him most.

THE PATRIARCH CONTINUES TO BE HEARD

He could not tolerate having the company in debt, and he was delighted when a *Forbes* magazine article on the company's progress under Philip Hofmann's leadership commented that Johnson & Johnson "doesn't owe anybody a dime." That, and a Hofmann quote – "We try to be dynamic in research, manufacturing, and marketing and sales, and ultraconservative financially" – warmed Johnson's heart.

Hofmann was doing a credible job as Johnson's successor, which the *Forbes* article pointed out. Even more important to the General, though, was that the present management was preserving and building on the culture that he had spent so many years creating and nurturing within the company. That aspect of the business was paramount to Johnson, who made his intent clear: "I am leaving a business, not money, and it is of great importance to me to maintain the integrity and personality of the company."

In the role of patriarch, Johnson was exercising as much restraint as possible to keep from interfering with routine decisions. He tried to stay away from that area, and for the most part he did. But through his endless storm of memos – the "blue blizzard" – he would advise and counsel, cajole, nudge, push, and occasionally intimidate, until he got his point across. He was crafty in his variety of approaches, but so was Hofmann, who had developed a technique for dealing with the General. "At times he could be exceedingly dogmatic, and therefore difficult," said Hofmann. "When he took a stubborn position, I wouldn't oppose him on the spot. I'd let it rest a few days, then come back and say, 'Now, General, let's review that matter again.' And if I had a logical argument, he would always listen and often change his position. It was how you approached it."

Johnson had once chided Hofmann about his lack of humility, an occasion that Hofmann recalled with amusement. "The General came to me and said: 'Phil, you have all this ability

82

and drive and punch, but you don't have enough humility.' Now, he thought *he* was humble because he felt that's how he should be. But he wasn't humble. He and I had the same problem with humility, and people with certain characteristics often do. Humility didn't fit him any more than it did me."

Johnson was clearly enjoying his new role as patriarch, philosopher, planner, and, in the view of some, royal second-guesser. He summed up for a friend how he saw his involvement in the business: "An important segment of my time is spent stopping some people from committing suicide. Another segment is spent identifying opportunities others do not grasp, but which offer progress, better service, and more profit, yet do not require great investment."

About the time of his seventy-first birthday, in April 1964, Johnson's associates began noticing a change in him. He had always been impatient, but now it was more noticeable. One colleague noted: "When he wanted something done, he wanted it done yesterday." Another said: "He was becoming quite a different person, perhaps attributable to his poor health and advancing age. He may have come to the inevitable realization that at some point you begin to lose your leadership. He was getting more and more irascible."

For the first time, Johnson began discussing the future of the company after his death, and the process for selecting a Chairman to succeed Hofmann someday. He also spoke about being tired and about how much he looked forward to returning to the sea on his next boat so he could sail it around the world to visit his companies. Tired or not, he would make it a "working ship."

TOOK ONE VOYAGE ON THE PILGRIM

All of his adult life Johnson owned boats and frequently commented, "I am most relaxed when I am at sea." And there was ample proof of that. About the time he stepped down as chairman he commissioned a shipyard in Scotland to build the 140-foot Pilgrim, a handsome vessel that encountered horrendous seas on its maiden voyage – with Johnson aboard – to the Canary Islands. Blaming the ship instead of the weather, Johnson decided to sell it before its anchor was dropped. He stepped off the ship at dockside, walked away and never looked back.

His next and final "working ship" was the Golden Crest, 190 feet long with a steel hull and built as an Army mine planter, or ACM 12, for active duty in the Harbor Defense Forces at the Panama Canal. After extensive refitting it became Johnson's "Dream Ship" which made several voyages worldwide in the final three years of his life and took him to many of Johnson & Johnson's far flung companies. He always presented himself as a guest but wound up involving himself in various business decisions, none of them of major importance.

HABIT OF DROPPING IN UNANNOUNCED

On his visits to international companies, he occasionally dropped in on a meeting unannounced and took a seat at the back of the room. Once when he did this and his presence was acknowledged, he told the group: "I'll have nothing to say at this meeting. Just go ahead." One manager recalled what happened next: "In no time, he was on his feet gesturing and making points, and soon he was completely involved in the discussion. He couldn't help himself."

At higher-level management meetings during his visits, the General would discuss many aspects of Johnson & Johnson's corporate philosophy. He seldom referred to the Credo, however, because it was hanging on the wall for all to see and, in his view, there was no compromise when it came to those responsibilities. He probably thought he was contributing to key business decisions more than he actually was, not realizing that his very presence was the most important contribution he could make.

After a long voyage he would often fly home to "catch up on things" at the office. After a short while he would fly back to the ship and continue his carefully planned journey to other Johnson & Johnson locations.

REFLECTING ON STOCK OWNERSHIP

In early January 1967, Johnson wrote his brother, Seward, his closest confidant: "I've been thinking a great deal of the future management and control of Johnson & Johnson. As a matter of fact, you know that this has been uppermost in my mind for a lifetime.

"At one point you and I owned in excess of eighty percent of the stock, I think at its highest point it was eighty-six percent. Since then, through good efforts and an attempt to do what we can for others, we have built trusts for children, trusts for charity, a trust for this, that and the other. In most of this we have tried to protect the continuity and competence of management but, nevertheless, we have engineered a very considerable dilution. Then came the great step after the war where we made the mistake of issuing stock and putting a portion of the company holdings on the open stock market.

"Now we must give great attention to an era that has developed, namely control and continuity. I hope you will think about this carefully and whenever the question arises do everything you can to give us the solidity of the closely held corporation we once had. I doubt that we can ever attain the majority at our highest point, but we should at all times be sure that we have as close to seventy percent of the stockholders with us as sooner or later there is going to be some kind of raid or organization engineered by those who, for one reason or another, dislike us. "This sort of thing is as old as man himself. The beneficiary bites off the hand of his benefactor."

HIS THOUGHTS ON THE RWJ FOUNDATION

Johnson had already decided that the bulk of his own stock holdings would go to The Robert Wood Johnson Foundation, though he did no advance planning for the dramatic expansion of the Foundation following his death. An associate explained Johnson's thinking:

"The target he clearly defined for the Foundation was that it be used to improve health care in the United States. He had great faith and confidence in his executives, those that he had put on the Foundation board, and he relied on their judgment. He didn't dictate what was to be done, but he had confidence that it would be done right. In his mind he felt 'I cannot control this thing from the grave,' so he placed his confidence and trust in his colleagues to produce the results he would have wanted.

MOUNTING CONCERNS ABOUT HIS HEALTH

In the early months of 1967, there was some concerned speculation about Johnson's health. He was quiet about it himself, but others were worried. One colleague later commented: "Looking back, I believe the General knew that his health was much worse than he led us to believe." At the time, the nation was embroiled in the war in Vietnam, and Johnson wrote to a friend: "I do my job each day the best way that I can, and close my mind to much else. This may be a cowardly view, but I ease my conscience as I have done my tour of duty in public, military and political life, and still stand ready for emergency and crisis service to the extent of my physical capacity." There was still a spark of his old energy there, and he was going on seventy-four.

As it turned out, Johnson had twelve months of life left.

If he sensed that he was failing, he made no attempt to slow his pace or confine his activity. If anything, an urgency crept into his schedule – the things he did and how he went about doing them. His first priority was to board the *Golden Crest* to continue his worldwide "inspection" of Johnson & Johnson companies. He took particular pride in the dramatic growth of the company overseas, because forty years earlier he had planted the seeds of the global business when he embarked on a world journey to explore new markets. In some respects, this was a retracing of that pioneering venture, and it probably added to his sense of accomplishment to see firsthand how the business had grown.

Four generations of Robert Wood Johnsons

OUR CREDO

We believe our first responsibility is to the doctors, nurses and patients, to mothers and fathers and all others who use our products and services. In meeting their needs, everything we do must be of high quality. We must constantly strive to reduce our costs in order to maintain reasonable prices. Customers' orders must be serviced promptly and accurately. Our suppliers and distributors must have an opportunity to make a fair profit.

We are responsible to our employees, the men and women who work with us throughout the world. Everyone must be considered as an individual. We must respect their dignity and recognize their merit. They must have a sense of security in their jobs. Compensation must be fair and adequate, and working conditions clean, orderly and safe. We must be mindful of ways to help our employees fulfill their family responsibilities. Employees must feel free to make suggestions and complaints. There must be equal opportunity for employment, development and advancement for those qualified. We must provide competent management, and their actions must be just and ethical.

We are responsible to the communities in which we live and work and to the world community as well. We must be good citizens – support good works and charities and bear our fair share of taxes. We must encourage civic improvements and better health and education. We must maintain in good order the property we are privileged to use, protecting the environment and natural resources.

Our final responsibility is to our stockholders. Business must make a sound profit. We must experiment with new ideas. Research must be carried on, innovative programs developed and mistakes paid for. New equipment must be purchased, new facilities provided and new products launched. Reserves must be created to provide for adverse times. When we operate according to these principles, the stockholders should realize a fair return.

Johnson & Johnson

RWJ in his office with daughter Sheila's photo on shelf

The new Chairman, Philip B. Hofmann,
tours the baby products plant

Richard B. Sellars, who succeeded Hofmann as Chairman,
and RWJ

The Board of Directors as honorary pallbearers

The Robert Wood Johnson Foundation in Princeton, N.J.

Maker of Tylenol Discontinuing All Over-Counter Drug Capsules

Offers to Replace Them After Woman's Death From Poisoned Pills

By ROBERT D. McFADDEN

Johnson & Johnson yesterday discontinued the manufacture and sale of all its over-the-counter medications in capsule form to prevent the kind of tampering that recently killed a woman who took cyanide-laced capsules of Extra-Strength Tylenol.

The company also offered, at its expense, to replace about 15 million packages of its capsule products in stores and homes across the nation with caplets, which are oval-shaped tablets coated to make them easier to swallow. It said it hoped to rebuild the lost capsule market in less tamper-prone caplets and tablets.

The phamaceutical concern, which markets scores of products and had sales of $6.4 billion last year, estimated that its withdrawal from capsules would cost $100 million to $150 million, after taxes. This will include the expenses of replacing six kinds of capsules already on the market and of retooling its plants as well as other costs in trying to rebuild its market position.

'Standards of Responsibilit'

"We feel the company ca~ guarantee the safety .~ ~egree consistent ~~ ~~anda~

The New York Times/William E. Sauro

James E. Burke, chairman of Johnson & Johnson, at news conference with large model of oval-shaped tablet known as a caplet.

(from page 1 of *The New York Times*)

The decision in 1986 to discontinue selling all over-the-counter capsules was based on following the Credo guidelines

AT SEA ABOARD THE *GOLDEN CREST*

For someone who had been a lifelong slave to perfection, Johnson found the *Golden Crest* a formidable challenge, but one he was clearly enjoying. By now, everything on the ship that was replaceable – or could be duplicated – had been replaced or duplicated. There were three radar systems and, as Johnson wrote, "enough radio on the bridge to confuse everybody." He added, "But, I figure some of it will work at times."

Earlier he had told Seward: "I am unalterably determined to bring this ship to perfect condition" – a pledge that Seward, knowing his brother, was sure would never be kept. Soon after leaving Curaçao, he reported again to Seward: "She is a strong, able, hard working deep sea ship. She is going well, but we still have a few major jobs ahead of us. We are running a happy ship and nearly all the men are competent." Certainly not perfection, but, for the General, pretty close. He signed off to Seward: "Take care of yourself, kid." The sea made boys of both of them.

A CLOSE RAPPORT WITH THE BRAZILIANS

Johnson was greeted warmly when he arrived in São Paulo, Brazil, where the company was headquartered. They were fond of him, and some time later a Brazilian manager explained why:

"Brazilians are emotional, and they like people with personality and flair. We admire these traits, and on his visits here he always made a strong impression. We embraced the Credo he wrote because no one had ever conducted a business here under these kinds of guidelines. His philosophy of running a business and treating people the way he did was totally different. Spotless plants and manicured lawns were uncommon. He was referred to here as 'our beloved General Johnson.'"

In São Paulo, Johnson stayed at the Hotel Cadoro, and years later the manager there remembered his visit: "General Johnson was planning a dinner for the local managers and their wives, and when he came to me to choose the menu, he asked if I knew how to cut lettuce for the salad. I said I thought we did, we had been cutting it for years. He wasn't convinced, so an hour before dinner he came down to the kitchen and demonstrated to the chef and me just how he wanted the lettuce sliced. He cut it on a diagonal. I'll never forget it."

In Brazil he helped resolve the important question of moving more of the company's manufacturing to São José dos Campos, away from overcrowded São Paulo. After inspecting the production line, he decided that the baby powder was a shade off-color and had to be corrected, and that the package design should be improved.

DISPLACED BY A WANDERING COCKROACH

As the ship headed for Trinidad, and a meeting with the manager of the tiny Johnson & Johnson company there, the General made plans for his visit. Meanwhile, Alan Donawa, a Trinidad native, just recently named manager there, awaited his arrival with some trepidation. Friends in the company had warned him about the perils of the visit from Johnson. Donawa made sure there was no greeting party when the *Golden Crest* docked at the U.S. Navy wharf on March 26, but, as instructed by telex, he was at the ship at eight o'clock the next morning. The events that followed were etched in his memory, especially the horror of the sauntering cockroach during the General's inspection of the tiny production line.

"I had been alerted about the General's passion for cleanliness," Donawa recalled, "and I thought I had prepared well. The day before his arrival, I had the exterminator in. The girls' uniforms were sparkling white. We were standing next to the production line, and out of the corner of my eye I spot this cockroach casually walking across the top of a package and heading for the General's line of sight. I'm hoping to God he doesn't see this thing. I knew immediately that I should have had the exterminator in weeks earlier – all we did was stir them up. Very carefully, I made two attempts to flick the thing away. He

94

turned to me and quietly said: 'Is this the sort of thing you get down here?' Then, when the inspection was over he said: 'Mr. Donawa, I don't think this is the place for you or the kind of place where we would like to manufacture. Tomorrow we will look for a new plant.'

"He ordered a car and driver and early the next morning we toured all around Port of Spain so he could get the feel of the place. After about three hours, he spotted a vacant building, and said: 'Mr. Donawa, I think this is an ideal location for our business.' It was a large building – very large – with ceilings about forty feet high. Very much larger than what we had. He said: 'I don't care if we have to pay dual rent. We will move here.' Here I am, new to the company, with no approval from my line management to move to a new plant, and now I will have two plants. I thought about it all the way back to my office on Sackville Street – yes, Sackville Street. I later signed a lease, and we moved, and it was a very nice location. I heard rumors of grumbling from New Brunswick, but no direct complaints."

KEEPING AN EYE ON THE FOLLOW-UP FILE

After flying back to New Brunswick, the General resumed his work schedule. The time away had not dulled the barb of his humor. After consulting his follow-up list, he realized that he had not received a response to a much earlier suggestion and wrote the tardy associate: "When I graduated from Kindergarten in short pants I wrote you about this. I am now a grown man. What happened?" And he still could not refrain from involving himself in every facet of the business. When he learned that a physician who had treated him was entering the hospital, he wrote him: "As long as you are going there, why not do some practical product testing for us?" He then sent the doctor a supply of disposable pillowcases and asked for a report on them – which he eventually got. In his role as chairman of the finance committee, his message – reduce costs wherever possible, and build up cash reserves – had not changed. When his recommendations met resistance, he offered this advice: "Twenty-five years from now, those in charge will be glad we acted in such a manner. If this seems painful to you now, I remind you that almost everything worthwhile is at times painful."

HIS HEALTH GROWS WORSE

Johnson was now tiring earlier in the day, so he decided to see Dr. T. Scudder Winslow at Roosevelt Hospital in New York for a checkup. "The x-rays came about quite accidentally," Nurse Ferretti recalled. "He was in the waiting room, and one of the radiologists whom he had consulted earlier stopped to say hello. When the General described how he felt, and the pain he was getting in his shoulder blade, the radiologist suggested an x-ray." They discovered a small tumor on the lobe of his left lung. He took the news stoically.

"For good or bad," he wrote Seward, "Dr. Winslow and I have decided to dismiss surgery (dangerous because of his heart condition), and we will begin treatment at once with anti-tubercular medication. After three weeks, we will x-ray the lung again. This, of course, leaves open the question of the lesion being benign or carcinogenic. I am told it is in an inaccessible spot and cannot be biopsied."

For the next several weeks he kept a hectic schedule visiting six of the company's textile plants in the South, including Chicopee Village, near Gainesville, Georgia. It was there in 1926, that Johnson had built the world's most modern textile mill and a 200-home village for employees. A few years back the company had sold the village, and in a report Johnson wrote to the Board of Directors on his visit he lamented that decision, of which he had been a part. He had taken a nostalgic stroll through Chicopee Village and noted: "The sidewalks are going, the streets are breaking up and many of the house roofs need repair." It was a painful sight and condition for what had once been one of his proudest and most innovative accomplishments.

When x-rays showed no improvement, it was decided that he should undergo treatment by lineal accelerator at the Ravdin Clinic at the University of Pennsylvania Hospital in Philadelphia.

The radiation therapy would be given to him six days a week for a period of five weeks, and he began it in early June. His uppermost concern appeared to be the adjustments he would have to make in his work schedule, but he resolved that problem. Because he was an outpatient, he was able to take up residence at the nearby Barclay Hotel, go to the hospital for treatment in the morning, and return to the hotel to carry on his day's work.

It was highly unlikely that the General could spend time at a hospital without attempting to make some changes. He kept his record intact in Philadelphia. "The first thing he did was revamp the nursing service at the hospital," a colleague said later. While this was an exaggeration, Johnson spent many hours each day conferring with the nurses and the hospital management. When he met a nurse supervisor from the Philippines who impressed him, he began exploring ways to bring more Philippine nurses to the hospital.

After five weeks of radiation treatments, Johnson was fatigued. "I am only operating on a few cylinders," he admitted. But his spirits were sent soaring when the final x-rays disclosed that the lesion was practically eliminated. "All of the specialists are pleased. . . . I am one of the lucky ones," he wrote jubilantly.

PLANS TO CONTINUE THE WORLD JOURNEY

He left that day for home, to finalize plans for the last leg of the world journey that would complete his personal inspection of Johnson & Johnson's major facilities, this time in Europe. The *Golden Crest* had proceeded to Amsterdam and was awaiting his arrival.

From Amsterdam, the *Golden Crest* would sail down the English Channel to the Bay of Biscay and into the Atlantic, making stops at La Coruña, Spain; Lisbon, Portugal; Gibraltar; Cagliari on the island of Sardinia; and then Naples, Italy. Next the ship would continue back through the Mediterranean Sea, stopping again in Spain and Gibraltar before heading for the Madeira Islands and then across the Atlantic to the final destination, Port of Spain, Trinidad.

The journey would be a long one. Unknown to anyone but the captain, Johnson had a simple wood coffin placed in the hold of the ship and had designated certain passages from the Bible to be read should he die when the *Golden Crest* was far from port.

When the ship docked at Gibraltar, the General was confronted with a new problem – trying to get three of his crew out of jail. While riding in the ship's launch, they had entered Spanish waters by mistake and were arrested by Spanish authorities. The launch was confiscated, and they spent the night in jail before Johnson and the captain were able to negotiate their release. "This is one of the vicissitudes of foreign travel," he wrote. But he had a few choice words about Generalissimo Francisco Franco, the Spanish dictator. "As for Franco," he wrote, "I wouldn't start a St. Bernard farm in Spain. The place is almost as bad as Cuba."

The General was especially pleased with the new plant outside of Rome and its classic Roman architecture – which he had approved earlier. He described the architecture as "grand," but he decided the acoustics in the executive dining room were bad and suggested carpeting would help – a hard, wearable carpet." As he drove around the grounds, he dictated a memo suggesting places where seeding and new shrubbery were needed. Also unhappy with the appearance of a cement drainage ditch that passed under the entrance road to the administration building, he recommended that it be refaced. All in all, the Italian plant manager escaped virtually unscathed, compared with other new plant inspections. (Johnson once described a new plant in Scotland as "ghastly.")

FATIGUED, BUT HE TOOK HIS WATCH ON THE BRIDGE

The world journey was now almost completed, and in a span of just over two years Johnson had logged more than 35,000 miles on the *Golden Crest* and had managed to visit most Johnson & Johnson companies around the world. At times during this final part of the voyage he became bone weary, but he was still standing watch on the bridge. That was important to him. He complained little about his health, and for reasons he did not explain – perhaps it was a sense of fatalism – he had not arranged to have a physician aboard for this trip, as he had for the others. His spirits were high as the ship cleared Gibraltar and headed south, to pick up the trade winds and begin its long voyage across the South Atlantic. The longer trips gave him more time to think.

"This letter finds us two-thirds of the way across the southern Atlantic," he wrote. "The sea is calm, with a very mild swell. The ship has worked well. She adheres to schedule and navigates straight as an arrow. She is, without question, the best ship in the world of her type." It was the most glowing report he had ever given from the *Golden Crest*. To a friend in Bermuda, he wrote: "At long last I am really proud of this ship. I am sure that we have the best long-range private vessel in the world. It seems strange, but no other vessel is doing what we do. Even those with large yachts really don't take them to sea."

LETTERS TO ROCKEFELLER AND REAGAN

Arriving home in late September, the General began catching up on the political news. A few days later he wrote Nelson Rockefeller, then governor of New York: "This morning on the radio I learned of the Reagan-Rockefeller or Rockefeller-Reagan ticket. Either way, this scheme gives me great enthusiasm. I know you said that you will not take it, however, this country is in such a mess that you may have to make the sacrifice."

He wrote essentially the same letter to Ronald Reagan, then governor of California, saying he would support the ticket with either man heading it. The General had liked Reagan since he first entered politics and began lashing out against communism in televised speeches. Once he sent for a thousand copies of a Reagan speech, "A Time for Choosing," along with a message that said, in part: "I have rather vague plans of working for you. . . ." Reagan wrote back that he would be grateful for any help.

MANAGING SMALL COMPANIES "A PROBLEM"

Shortly after his return – and after reflecting on what he had learned from his world tour – Johnson shared his observations with the Executive Committee in several memos. While he remained a strong proponent of decentralization, he said, he had found some flaws in that philosophy. "We have yet to learn how best to operate small companies. We are a large family of small industries, and we become large only when we put them all together. We must think in terms of managing small and medium-size companies. . . . We have a fine management, but we must constantly improve." Then in a company-by-company evaluation, he used his familiar metaphors: companies "in intensive care" or "in the repair shop." He was particularly concerned about countries that had erected political and economic barriers to growth of the business. "Should we diminish the business? Should we quietly fade away?" In his franker moments, he confessed that he was happier when there were some problems. "It gives me some things to fix," he would say.

ONCE HOME THE INSPECTIONS CONTINUED

It was only a matter of time before the General resumed his inspection rounds of Johnson & Johnson companies in the New Brunswick area. "We are roaming outside your building," began one memo, followed by a critique of the exterior paint and the "scar" in the landscaping. He took the same trip twice on the Pennsylvania Railroad before concluding that a new warehouse was "cheap looking" and that the exterior had to be changed. So did the American flag in front of the building – it was too small.

Parking lots bothered him greatly. "Most people do not recognize that a parking lot should be a part of the architectural and landscaping design of a fine property," he wrote. "Unfortunately, car parking has become a very great liability to many otherwise fairly good industrial properties. Parking lots are also ruining the appearance of college campuses, hospitals and churches." Driving by a new elevated parking lot near the home office, he could see "the tops of motor cars" so he had a two-and-a-half-foot wall built to screen the cars from the street below. After an early snowfall, a sidewalk plow threw snow against the red brick of Johnson Hall, and it stuck to the side of the building, creating what he felt was an eyesore. "If they have forgotten how to use a shovel, ask someone from the retired list of pensioners and they'll tell you," he suggested.

RWJ REFLECTS ON THE CREDO

In some respects, Johnson was conducting a reprise of his life's work. He reminded his successor, Philip Hofmann, of the origins of the Credo: "We devoted much thought to the phraseology. Our attempt was to simplify a brief document that we believed could be understood, could be used as a declaration of our policy and principles straight down to the bench level in all of our facilities worldwide." He got the idea to translate the Credo into various languages and sending it as a New Year's greeting card to every company employee worldwide, but when he learned how much it would cost he thought better of it.

His medical problems had now grown more serious. The pains in his shoulder blades and around his lungs were recurring more frequently, and he had developed a persistent cough. He returned to the University of Pennsylvania Hospital for five days. During that time, he was diagnosed as having a possible pulmonary embolus (a foreign body that occludes a blood vessel), and after he left the hospital he was required to have medication injected into his abdomen every six hours. For the next few weeks, he gave himself many of the injections. "This is the price of staying alive," he wrote. He dreaded that he might have cancer. As for surgery, he would not consider it.

In late November, Johnson began making plans for another voyage, which he said would depart on February 1 for Jamaica, Puerto Rico, Barbados, Venezuela, and Colombia. He wrote his newspaper friend, Frank Farrell, who agreed to go along, as did Philip "Flip" Cochran, a friend from his days in Washington twenty-five years earlier. All three had a lot to talk about from the old days. "I was looking forward to the trip," Farrell said, "but unaware of the severity of his illness. The General loved the sea more than anything else in life, and he had the courage of a pirate."

THE MEDICAL TESTS BECOME ALARMING

In the coming weeks, which would be the last of his life, Johnson's courage and tenacity would be tested as never before. Spells of tiredness and weakness were now recurring with greater frequency, and not being able to pinpoint the cause frustrated him. He was also feeling pain more often, but not in the same places, and this made self-diagnosis – a practice he often indulged in – more difficult. On his notepad, he kept track of the times pain came and went, but there was no pattern to it, and this baffled him.

It took more than a perplexing medical condition to dampen his spirits when there were everyday problems to be solved. Over Thanksgiving weekend, the basement of the house in Princeton became flooded. Unable to find a plumber because of the holiday, Johnson took charge and, in his words, "laid out a scheme to correct the problem," which also included "reorganization of the household staff." Back in the office the following Monday, he wrote a friend that he had gone from the problem of a leaking pipe to the one dealing with "the world's dislocation of currency." "So you can see, it's going to be a nice, easy day," he added, with good spirit.

Johnson woke up in the early morning hours of Christmas in great discomfort. "Awakened with abdominal pain that roams around my midriff," he wrote on his bedside notepad. His pain medication offered some relief, but two nights later he was awakened again by "semi-acute pain just under the right shoulder blade towards the spine." In what was more wishful thinking than an accurate diagnosis, he scribbled in his notepad: "Am thinking it may be rheumatic or arthritic." On New Year's Day, he reported pain when taking a deep breath and speculated that it might be pleurisy. On January 2, he requested that the company plane come to Florida to take him north, for he had decided to be admitted to Roosevelt Hospital in New York.

At the hospital, the doctors began a series of tests and put him on medication. After a few days he seemed to snap back, finding fault with the hard pillows, a malfunctioning light in the bathroom, and the inquisitive nature of the interns and residents making grand rounds. He sent Nurse Olga Ferretti out to purchase new pillows – "We'll use them again." – he noted, to justify the purchase. He got the hospital to fix the bathroom light promptly, and he persuaded the doctors to skip him on grand rounds. Clearly, he was feeling more like his old self.

ALWAYS IN CHARGE EVEN THOUGH HOSPITALIZED

Redesigning the hospital bed also perked him up. Hospital beds were very uncomfortable and poorly designed, he complained, and his in particular. He spent hours sketching and providing the details of a new type of hospital bed that he believed would be far superior. Evie had come up from Florida to be with him, and on one of her visits he proudly showed her the sketches. This one was longer, and earlier he had maintained that all hospital beds should first be tested by the Green Bay Packers football team.

Having solved the hospital bed problem, he looked around for others.

After reading the newspapers one morning, he placed a call to New Jersey Governor Richard J. Hughes. The governor remembered it well: "He phoned me from the hospital to raise hell about something the Port of New York Authority had done, or did wrong, or failed to do – I forget exactly what, but it involved the interests of New Jersey, so Bob Johnson was involved." And at 4:30 one morning he wrote a memo to the chairman of The Robert Wood Johnson Foundation about a new plan he had for medical scholarships. Two days later, he outlined his views on the problems facing the nation's hospitals: "I have been striving for some time to identify the problems facing hospitals, and I think I am getting close to it." It was almost business as usual and, except for the medical reports, there might have been room for optimism.

Seward came to the hospital to visit his brother. It was a tearful meeting and Seward left weeping like a child. Johnson wanted no other visitors, except Evie. In those final days, Evie and Johnson drew closer than they had ever been. "The only one he then wanted there was Mrs. Johnson," Nurse O'Neal said. "In the agony of his last days, he wanted her near him. She was understanding, and he leaned on her – and that said volumes to me."

Once again the General took his notepad and heavy black pencil and began making notations about his worsening condition. He dutifully jotted down the times he felt the pains – as though he was recording them in a ship's log – and as the seas became more turbulent the letters in each word became shakier.

HIS DEATH WAS PEACEFUL

It was a few minutes before six on Tuesday evening, January 30, and Nurses Dorothy O'Neal and Mary Feaster were on duty at the General's bedside. Nurse O'Neal recounted what happened: "He reached his arm out in front of him, and I took it to steady him. Mary took his other hand in hers. Then his head fell on my shoulder, and that was it. He died."

He died at 6:03 p.m., though the General would have recorded it as 1803.

Philip Hofmann was patiently keeping vigil in the hospital waiting room and was the one to telephone New Brunswick with the news, and that call put in motion the plans that had been made earlier. Johnson's obituary, which this author had written weeks earlier, was released to the news media by the corporate public relations department.

HIS WISH FOR A SIMPLE FUNERAL

It came as no great surprise to anyone who knew him that the General had left explicit instructions for his funeral and burial. They read as follows:

> It is my wish that my funeral will be a simple procedure. In the days when we had one plant and I knew all the people it would have been appropriate to close down the units of Johnson & Johnson for a day as a tribute to my name. I do not consider this appropriate now. Therefore, I request that this should not be done.
>
> I further request that my remains should not be on view in any funeral parlor nor at my home. As soon as possible the casket should be placed in the chapel of my church, Christ Church in New Brunswick. The pallbearers, honorary and otherwise, will be the Board of Directors of Johnson and Johnson.
>
> Miscellaneous flowers should be avoided. The casket can be draped with one flower blanket. I do not wish a eulogy. A competent organist may be employed, but I do not wish any other form of music, such as a voice. The officiating minister is to use the classic service of the church. The ceremony at the mausoleum will be brief.
>
> I will be deeply pleased if those who have worked with me for years are present in addition to the members of my family.

Colleagues were troubled by Johnson's request that there be no eulogy, so the night he died this author was asked to write a tribute to the General and have it ready for review the next morning. Summarizing his life and accomplishments in a few hundred words seemed like a daunting assignment at the time. The following morning it was presented for review, and, as inadequate as it now seems, it was approved as written, with no changes. The decision was to call it a "tribute" as opposed to a "eulogy," to justify going counter to Johnson's wishes. No one believed that he would have been persuaded to change his mind, but they also knew that this time there would be no memo from him.

Fearing that his death might have an impact on the company stock because of his large personal holdings, Johnson had taken precautions to avoid that by writing an announcement to be distributed after his death. It read:

> To Whom It May Concern:
> In recent years a goal of General Johnson was the arrangement of his affairs in such a way that his death would not adversely affect Johnson & Johnson, its employees or its stockholders. To this end, he stressed within Johnson & Johnson the development of outstanding management. He arranged his personal financial affairs in such a way that a sale of Johnson & Johnson stock at the time of his death would not be necessary to pay expenses, bequests and taxes. We are advised by counsel that he succeeded in his endeavor and that the sale of Johnson & Johnson stock is neither necessary nor contemplated.

As one of the executors of Johnson's estate, Philip Hofmann was present when Johnson's safe deposit box was opened. "I lifted the first document out of the box and it was a U.S. Treasury bond for $1 million. It was meticulously planned. It wasn't necessary to sell a single share of Johnson & Johnson stock to pay the inheritance tax. All of his stock went to The Robert Wood Johnson Foundation, other than what was for his family and Evie and the trusts he had set up."

The funeral service was held on a rainy Friday morning, February 2. Christ Church was filled to capacity with family members, friends, public officials from afar, and a large representation from Johnson & Johnson, but many fewer than wanted to attend. The General got most of his final wishes. There were no flowers other than those draping the coffin. There was no vocalist. The twenty-three members of the Board of Directors – all of them his executives – were serving as honorary pallbearers. The service was brief and simple. Reverend Newberry rose to read the tribute, which Johnson certainly would have edited had he been given the chance.

THE TRIBUTE

Robert Wood Johnson was a very unusual man. Many of us will live an entire lifetime and never know another man quite like him.

He was born with opportunity, which sometimes has a tendency to spoil a man. Opportunity didn't spoil Robert Wood Johnson; instead, he used it to enrich his own life and the lives of an untold number of people who were fortunate enough to win his friendship or his admiration, or his concern.

He was born with a restless energy that was amazing to behold. It often left the people around him breathless and disbelieving, and perhaps capriciously, this stirred him to even greater effort.

Robert Wood Johnson possessed a tenacity of spirit that few men could match, and seldom was he without a challenger. But once he set his sights on a goal, there was very little doubt that he would achieve it. Even when he lost, he still managed to be philosophical.

Dignity was a characteristic that accompanied him all through his life. It was apparent in his bearing, in his appearance and in his manner. Yet he had a disarming wit that he loved to call into play at precisely the moment when it was least expected.

While other men were preoccupied by the past and the present, his thoughts always seemed to be probing the future – new ideas, new projects, an agile and adventurous mind that always seemed to function best when spurred by a sense of urgency. Great men have always been frugal with time, and Robert Johnson was no exception. For him, there always seemed to be so much to do, and never quite enough time in which to do it.

Of all the qualities that this unusual man possessed, none served the world better than the tender concern he had for those less privileged than he. The spirit of giving, not only of himself but of his worldly goods, has reached out and touched countless numbers of people in the far corners of the earth. It is impossible to comprehend all of the good that he did for his fellow men during his lifetime, and this is Robert Johnson's greatest legacy. His deeds are forever inscribed on the hearts of those to whom he was benefactor.

Perhaps his most inspired devotion was directed toward the men and women with whom he worked. He invested them with a sense of dignity. He provided in abundance the material needs for them and for their families. He constructed buildings that established standards years before their time, and he had the wisdom to make the working conditions as modern as the structures themselves.

He left his imprint on the business world, the field of medical care, the political arena, and as a public servant, statesman, patriot, soldier and humanitarian. The surprising thing is not that he did so many things, but that he did them so well.

So now we come to the parting of ways, we who were privileged to be close to him through the years. Life is fleeting at best, but think how much better ours has been because we were fortunate enough to cross paths with Robert Wood Johnson. Remember him in these ways, and we will have been worthy of his friendship.

There is a brief passage from the Scriptures that speaks for Robert Wood Johnson:

I have fought the good fight, and have finished the course, I have run the race and have kept the faith.

When the service was over, the members of the Board of Directors left the church first and formed two lines. The bronze casket, which the General would have thought exorbitantly expensive, was wheeled between the two lines of directors to the hearse parked on Church Street. Standing four and five deep on the sidewalk across the street were scores of the old-timers from Johnson & Johnson, workers he had always considered friends. They had waited in the drizzling rain to bid him farewell.

The service at the family mausoleum was private and brief, just as Johnson had requested. One of his colleagues noted later: "After the funeral, we came right back to work." That surely would have pleased him.

THE CREDO'S ROLE IN THE TWO TYLENOL CRISES

What began as Johnson & Johnson's darkest hour turned out to be its brightest in terms of corporate reputation. In late September 1982, one or more crazed criminals – still unknown to authorities – used Tylenol Extra Strength Capsules as a murder weapon by lacing them with cyanide poison and killing seven innocent people. The method used was diabolical beyond belief. The murderers purchased eight bottles of Tylenol from five food and drug stores within a twenty-mile radius of Chicago. About fifty of the red-and-white capsules were pried open, and the powdered medication was mixed with potassium cyanide, a powerful poison in crystalline form. The lethal mixture was then put back in the capsules, which were reassembled and put back in the original bottles and outer boxes. Each repackaged bottle was then secretly placed back on the shelf in the same store where it had been purchased, to ensure that there would be no questions raised at the checkout counters when unsuspecting victims repurchased them later.

The first word of the horror came on the morning of September 30, when a reporter for the *Chicago Sun-Times* telephoned Johnson & Johnson's Corporate Public Relations Department and informed veteran staff member James A. Murray of a suspected link between Tylenol and the death of a Chicago-area woman from cyanide poisoning. The news was quickly passed along to the company's senior management, and they were stunned and disbelieving. About the same time, the Cook County medical examiner was giving the same shocking report to the medical director of the McNeil Consumer Products Company at Fort Washington, Pennsylvania, the makers of Tylenol products. McNeil is one of Johnson & Johnson's Family of Companies.

This ignited what came to be known as the "Tylenol Tragedy." It was later likened to throwing a lighted match into a vast, dry forest where an evil wind kept it burning fiercely for months. It was the greatest crisis of its kind ever to strike an American corporation.

The stunned disbelief in New Brunswick and Fort Washington rapidly turned to shocking reality. Within twenty-four hours, five women and two men from the Chicago area – all under thirty-six years of age – died painfully after ingesting the poisoned capsules in the belief that they were taking a pain remedy. Three of the dead were from the same family. After one brother had collapsed and died, his grief-stricken younger brother and his wife came to the dead man's apartment. Shaken and distraught, they sat down at the kitchen table and took capsules from the same poisoned bottle. They died too. And a twelve-year-old girl who had stayed home from school with a sore throat took one of the tainted capsules and died almost instantly.

The nation's news media converged on the story with frenzied intensity, putting it on the front pages of newspapers and at the top of television and radio newscasts – where it would remain for seemingly endless weeks. There was good cause for the alarm. For the first time ever, terrorism with lethal consequences had invaded the sanctity of the home, making everyone vulnerable. In *Life* magazine, Loudon Wainwright Jr. wrote: "The killer, in effect, had appeared in everyone's home – every medicine cabinet had become a potential hiding place for some life-threatening horror."

A cold chill swept over the executives of Johnson & Johnson and McNeil as they realized that the poisoning might have occurred in the plant during manufacturing. Tylenol was the nation's most popular brand of pain remedy, with more than one hundred million users. There were thirty-one million bottles of Tylenol capsules out there – in homes, schools, hospitals, and work places, and on the shelves of tens of thousands of retail outlets across the nation. How widespread was this murderous act? How many other lives were threatened?

PANDEMONIUM IN CHICAGO

In Chicago there was pandemonium. Police and fire vehicles moved through the streets blaring warnings about using the product, as police and company representatives moved from store to store in the area of the murders, removing Tylenol capsules from the shelves so they could be tested to determine whether they had been poisoned. And agents of the Food and Drug Administration descended on the McNeil plant in Pennsylvania, where the tainted capsules had been produced, searching for clues. There was desperate uncertainty about how the poisoning took place and how far the wicked plot might reach. Then it was learned that some of the tainted capsules had been produced at a McNeil plant in Round Rock, Texas. The likelihood of an in-plant tampering at two widely separated plants seemed slight. With this information in hand, authorities intensified the search for the killers in the Chicago area.

The alarm spread quickly to other countries. At Heathrow Airport outside London, and at Orly and Charles de Gaulle airports in France, loudspeakers warned passengers from the United States of the possible danger and instructed them to bring any Tylenol they had to a customs desk for inspection. In Italy, the warning was broadcast over state television. In markets as far apart as Poland, Guatemala, the Philippines, and Singapore, authorities issued warnings and removed Tylenol from store shelves. The problem was worldwide. Tylenol products were on the market in twenty-three countries.

J&J'S MOST IMPORTANT ACTION

The senior management of Johnson & Johnson took two early steps to protect the public: From the very first call, the company was completely open and forthright with the news media and began a phased voluntary withdrawal of Tylenol Capsules that would later become both nationwide and worldwide. Cooperation with the news media was seen as the most effective way to warn all consumers about the potential danger, even though there was no evidence that the plot had reached beyond Chicago. The fright and mounting anxiety had gripped the nation, and this alone was seen as reason enough to get the capsules off the market. Johnson & Johnson's reputation and credibility were at stake, as was the compelling need to protect the public.

The Federal Bureau of Investigation quickly entered the case, giving it the highest priority. Working with authorities in Pennsylvania, agents of the Food and Drug Administration, after careful investigation, declared that the poisoning had not taken place at the McNeil plant. It was virtually impossible to gain access to the product during the automated production process, and even if that had been possible, it would have taken nearly a ton of cyanide in the mixing vat to contaminate the product in the concentration found in the capsules in Chicago. There was prayerful thanks at the company, where the worst fears were that the poisoning had taken place in the plant.

While there was no tangible evidence that the poisoning plot extended beyond Chicago, there was no certainty of that. Speculation was rampant, and often fed by the latest headline or newscast, even when hard facts were missing. Poison-control centers were flooded with calls from frantic people who claimed they were feeling ill and suspected they had been poisoned. Sometimes there was a link to Tylenol, but not always. Six hysterical residents of the Pittsburgh area went to local hospitals after viewing a graphic television program that described the symptoms of cyanide poisoning. They were sure they had been poisoned. The emotional scene was replayed in towns and cities all across the nation. Pathologists were quick to point out that everyone's blood has traces of cyanide and that heavy smokers test four times higher, thereby complicating the procedure and prolonging the final results.

NATION IS ALARMED BY SUDDEN DEATHS

The cases of mistaken illness were troublesome to deal with, but not nearly as alarming as news of sudden deaths of some 250 people all across the nation linked in some way, no matter how tenuously, to the use of Tylenol. One example was the death of a trucker who died in the cab of his vehicle along a Tennessee highway. Police found a bottle of Tylenol capsules on the seat beside him. He was a heavy smoker and tested positive for cyanide, but doctors found that he had actually died of a heart attack. In time, all the other sudden deaths thought to be part of the Tylenol plot were attributed to other causes, mostly heart attacks and stroke, but they contributed to the growing volume of press coverage. While medical tests were being performed on the deceased, reporters kept the story alive, often calling the company and announcing: "We think we have another one here."

Both the FBI and the FDA initially opposed the company's decision to withdraw all capsules nationwide (four other capsule products were included in the recall), because that would be capitulating to the terrorist and would threaten the nation's system of marketing food and proprietary drug products. "Sick minds would be encouraged to repeat these acts," another said in arguing against the nationwide withdrawal. FBI Director William Webster was concerned that because Halloween was coming it might trigger a wave of copycat crimes. But a bizarre coincidence in California – where strychnine was put in Tylenol capsules in an unsuccessful poisoning plot – convinced them that Johnson & Johnson's decision was the right one.

"Someone was using our brand as a vehicle for murder, and we had to remove the vehicle," Burke said. The prompt action saved lives. Two of the eight bottles of Tylenol capsules containing cyanide were recovered in the Chicago area before they could claim more victims. One bottle was removed from a store shelf, another was returned by a very lucky woman who had purchased it but had yet to take any of the contaminated capsules. Given that an estimated fifty capsules had been poisoned, it was a miracle that the fiendish crime had claimed just seven victims.

Consumers who had purchased Tylenol capsules were urged to return them to a testing center or throw them away, and McNeil promised to replace the capsules with the tablet product, which was above suspicion. To be absolutely certain the solid tablet product was safe, a group of company scientists were later asked to see whether they could find a way to contaminate tablets. They did discover a way, but it involved the use of a hyperbaric chamber and a process only a scientist could carry out. Even disposing of the capsules posed a problem for some officials. In San Francisco, there were warnings about contaminating the city's sewer system.

INVESTIGATION GETS NOWHERE

Investigators in Chicago were working around-the-clock but making little headway. What few leads they had took them down one blind alley after another. There were conflicts among local, state, and federal authorities over jurisdiction, adding to the turmoil. The Illinois attorney general took charge of the investigation – and as if that wasn't enough pressure, he also had an election coming up. He appointed a Tylenol Task Force to cooperate in the investigation, and this group would grow to an unwieldy 170 members. The media claimed they got in each other's way. The headquarters for the investigation was a converted garage in Des Plaines, and there a band of edgy reporters impatiently sought new information on the case. They came from as far away as London.

Quiet grieving for the seven victims and their families was taking place within the company. Despite the frenzy of work generated by the crisis, expressions of deep sorrow for the misfortune of "those poor people" were heard everywhere. They came from those who had manufactured the product with pride, from those who had sold it with confidence, and from top-echelon executives who were still disbelieving. Letters of condolence were written to the families, but numerous suggestions to show the company's deep sense of regret in more tangible ways fell victim to the legal ramifications of such actions. It was not a popular course, but one that had to be adhered to. The fact that the company had been held blameless – and was itself a victim – would later nullify the legal actions that eventually came.

Despite the absence of leads, the combined weight of the Tylenol news coverage throughout the nation was staggering. From the outset, senior executives at both Johnson & Johnson and McNeil were available to the press for interviews and television appearances, even though they could shed no light on the mystery. Making the executives available served to strengthen the belief that the company was blameless and not resorting to the run-and-hide tactic that infuriates the news media. This approach strengthened the relationship with the press, which continued to show surprising sympathy for the company's plight.

The enterprising reporters who were pursuing new angles to the story kept it in each day's news and often on the front pages. The combined network news coverage was now averaging an hour of air time a day. The story had taken on a life of its own. It was later determined that the case had commanded more print space than any news story since the assassination of President John F. Kennedy in Dallas in 1963, and more television coverage since the reporting of the Vietnam War. Both the Associated Press and United Press International ranked Tylenol as the second impact story of the year – the first being the ongoing coverage of the American economy.

A seemingly endless flood of press calls came day and night to Johnson & Johnson's corporate public relations staff – all of whom were former journalists, familiar with news coverage and the ways of wily reporters. Over time, the number of calls from the news media exceeded 2,500. Beginning with the first call, a log was kept recording the name and phone number of every reporter who phoned. When information wasn't immediately available, the reporter received a return call. The same practice was followed at McNeil. No public relations agency people participated in this phase of the crisis. The record of reporters who were covering the story would prove invaluable later.

CEO JIM BURKE: "AN UNREMITTING NIGHTMARE"

Numerous false leads were pursued, and even those with no validity came back to haunt the company and prompted Burke to describe the situation as "an unremitting nightmare." Many of the suspicions that Tylenol capsules were involved in illness or death beyond the Chicago murders were totally unfounded. Scientists working on the investigation tried to emphasize that because cyanide absorbs water readily the gelatin that comprises the shell of a capsule contains water that would be quickly absorbed by the poison. Thus, a capsule containing cyanide would decompose and turn dark in a few weeks, making it easily recognizable as a contaminated capsule. Perhaps understandably, the scientific explanation was not very reassuring to most people.

One of the legitimate suspects that emerged in Chicago was a darkly brooding man with satanic symbols tattooed on his body and a predisposition to violence. When the police got a tip, they raided his apartment and found a horrifying collection of poisons and a guidebook on how to commit mass murder with them. It turned out, however, that the suspect had not been in Chicago at the time the Tylenol capsules were poisoned and placed on the store shelves. Enraged that a former co-worker had tipped off the police about him, the suspect killed the man he believed to be the informant – but he killed the wrong person. The newspapers in Chicago portrayed the bizarre mistake as an extension of the Tylenol tragedy, and now there were eight dead.

Suddenly there was an outbreak of brazen attempts at extortion, with Johnson & Johnson as the target. Conniving individuals thought they had found a way to make easy money by threatening to do more harm to the company by contaminating others of its products. In an attempt to catch one extortionist, an FBI agent, posing as a company executive, went to downtown Newark and boarded a bus. Following instructions in the extortion letter, he carried a briefcase supposedly containing a large amount of money, and as the bus passed a designated spot – a small park – the FBI agent threw the briefcase out the window, as the letter had instructed. Other FBI agents were nearby, disguised as workers. Several people descended on the briefcase lying on the ground in the park, but none of them was the extortionist. The trap had failed to catch its prey.

The only arrest ever made in the Tylenol case was a would-be extortionist. James W. Lewis, an unemployed accountant from Chicago, was apprehended in the New York Public Library after a stakeout by the FBI. It was yet another strange twist in an already bizarre investigation. Lewis had earlier been questioned about a murder in Kansas City before he moved to Chicago. After the Tylenol murders, he sent an extortion letter to Johnson & Johnson demanding $1 million to "stop the killing." The letter had been sent from New York, and investigators turned their attention to Manhattan in search of Lewis, who had also written letters to the *Chicago Tribune*.

THE THREAT TO THE WHITE HOUSE

When it became apparent that Lewis was reading the *Chicago Tribune* in New York City, the FBI began a surveillance of out-of-town newsstands and the New York Public Library. At the library, the FBI's patience paid off and Lewis was arrested. It turned out that Lewis had also written a letter to the White House, threatening to "bomb" it with plastic explosives dropped from a radio-controlled model airplane that Lewis said would be launched from a nearby park. It was a wild scheme, but it alarmed both the FBI and the Secret Service.

A few executives at Johnson & Johnson, working closely with the FBI, knew about the threatening letter to the White House but had been sworn to secrecy. Early one morning, James Litke, the Associated Press bureau chief in Chicago and one of the most tenacious reporters covering the murders, phoned Johnson & Johnson's vice president of public relations (the author) at home and asked bluntly: "What the hell is the Secret Service doing at the Tylenol Task Force?" (referring to the investigation meeting in Chicago). After a slight pause came the reply: "I don't know." It was the only time during the Tylenol episode that the press got an evasive response.

Lewis was convicted of extortion and served more than twelve years in prison. Investigators tried to implicate him in the Tylenol murders but could not make a case against him. Lewis stoutly defended his innocence in the murders, once telling Cable News Network: "It's just as impossible for me to be the Tylenol killer as it would be for me to be the killer of Julius Caesar." Lewis had been slated for parole earlier, but his letter in 1982, threatening the life of President Ronald Reagan, came back to haunt him, and the parole board decided he should serve his time.

The press had been inadvertently misled for several days early in the story when they asked the crucial question: Was cyanide used in the manufacturing process? After checking with production people, the reply was a flat "No." Investigators had asked the same question and were told the same thing. Several days later, the head of quality control at McNeil disclosed that a tiny amount of cyanide was indeed present in the testing lab, which was located in a building apart from the manufacturing plant. It was inconceivable that this small amount of cyanide could have been used in the murders – besides, none of it was missing. The issue was credibility, and Johnson & Johnson spokesmen had given their word. Almost immediately the Associated Press, the *New York Times*, and the *Newark Star-Ledger* learned of the error. In a display of journalistic fairness and responsibility, they noted the discrepancy well into the next day's stories, and discounted the importance of the presence of a small amount of cyanide in the testing lab.

Day in and day out the story dealt in tragedy, but every now and then a faint trace of humor emerged. A ten-year-old New Jersey boy wrote a carefully worded extortion letter to Johnson & Johnson, demanding payment of $1 million. He then put his home address on the envelope, and because he didn't have a stamp he gave it to his father to mail, which he dutifully did without suspecting the contents. The father was left to judge what punishment, if any, should be meted out.

THE DECISION TO BRING TYLENOL BACK

In addition to demonstrated marketing skills, Johnson & Johnson was known for having capable and competitive management. Once it was determined that the poisoning had not taken place in the plant, the marketing people began to discuss how to bring the Tylenol brand back. They turned to the marketer's stock-in-trade: consumer polling. The polls showed that while an astounding 99 percent of Americans were aware of the murders in Chicago, an encouraging 90 percent did not fault the company for what happened. This left the door open for the comeback that many of the marketing and advertising "experts" had already decided was impossible. They declared that the Tylenol brand was dead. In doing so, many even wrote off the tablet form, which posed no threats. Consumers had shown a strong preference for capsules over tablets because they saw them as being more like prescription medicine, which Tylenol was when first introduced by McNeil two decades earlier.

On the eighth day of the crisis, the decision was made to ignore the doomsayers and bring Tylenol capsules back, this time in tamper-resistant packaging that would ensure the product's safety. The groundwork had been laid to resurrect the $450 million business that had collapsed virtually overnight. Television advertising had been halted at the first word of the murders, so consumers would not be exposed to messages about pain relief when they were hearing newscasts linking the product to murder. The company promptly sent 450,000 telex messages to physicians, hospitals, and distributors, explaining the problem and seeking their confidence and support. Toll-free telephone lines were quickly set up by McNeil, and there were 136,000 calls from consumers seeking information about the poisonings, and thousands who offered moral support.

Everyone at the company knew that there were challenging days ahead. Burke put it clearly in a message to employees: "It will take time, it will take money, and it will be very difficult," he warned, "but we consider it a moral imperative, as well as good business, to restore Tylenol to its preeminent position." He went

119

to the McNeil plant in Pennsylvania, where employees crowded into the cafeteria to hear him deliver an emotion-charged speech that set the fighting tone for the recovery effort. Burke was especially adept at rallying people to perform beyond even their own expectations. That day, he was brilliant at it.

The employees of McNeil and Johnson & Johnson – even those not directly involved – got caught up in the recovery effort and volunteered their services. The entire families who showed up on weekends to help out were assigned to answer the banks of toll-free phones and speak to customers who called in to accept the offer of a free exchange of Tylenol tablets for capsules they had purchased. Many callers, and others as well, expressed their sympathy for the company. When a group of McNeil employees formed a morale-boosting committee, they came up with the slogan "We're Coming Back" and placed an order for lapel buttons with a California supplier. Two days later, enough "We're Coming Back" buttons for the entire work force arrived. "No charge," a note with the shipment said.

EXTRAORDINARY EFFORT AT McNEIL

Cooperation and goodwill came to Johnson & Johnson and McNeil from many sources. Even usually fierce competitors were reluctant to fill the empty store shelves with their pain-relief products – space only recently occupied by Tylenol capsules before they were swept away.

The technical problems associated with the design, manufacture, and installation of tamper-resistant packaging machinery were daunting. Early estimates were that it would take six months. Responding to McNeil's desperate need to get back on the market before memory of the product faded, outside suppliers of machinery and other production needs performed minor miracles in record time that no one thought was possible.

For generations, Johnson & Johnson had enjoyed a unique relationship with its millions of customers, a relationship that had a certain mystique. It went beyond a commitment to fulfill the responsibilities outlined in Robert Wood Johnson's Credo. There were other companies that performed admirably in these areas. And still, consumers consistently indicated in various studies that they had developed a special warm spot for the company that had been making Johnson's baby products for the better part of a century. It was not a marketing pipe dream, for the edge given Johnson & Johnson showed up time after time in consumer surveys. As best the company could determine, it was the role that the use of baby products played in strengthening the bond between generations of infants and their parents – mothers in particular.

Studies conducted by psychologists and pediatricians, and independent of the company's interests, had long ago determined the importance of "touch" in the development of an infant. Touch conveyed love and a sense of security. In applying powder, lotion, and other baby products to the infant, touch played an important role and helped to strengthen the bond between mother and infant. Other studies showed that the distinctive floral fragrance of Johnson's Baby Powder was one of the most familiar of all scents and that it always brought back pleasant memories of the warm relationship between a child and its mother. This, the believers said, was powerful reason to have trust in a company whose products could stimulate such a deeply personal response. Though not fully understanding the mystique, Johnson & Johnson welcomed the advantage it offered them in its relationship with the public. It was a bitter irony that the gentle, loving relationship between mother and child should somehow be a factor in the comeback phase of a crime of evil-minded brutality.

IMPACT OF THE "TRUST US" CAMPAIGN

If the public had trust and confidence in the company, as many believed, now was the time to draw on it. The first television advertising in the comeback was a brief campaign with one basic theme – "Trust Us" – and featured the medical director of McNeil, Dr. Thomas N. Gates, who had a calming, authoritative voice and could easily have passed for the family physician. From a professional office setting, Dr. Gates looked squarely at the camera and asked his audience to trust the company while it prepared to bring Tylenol back in tamper-resistant packaging.

The nation's news media immediately picked up on the "Trust Us" theme, and the commercials got wide attention in the news columns. To counsel him and help make key decisions, both in managing the crisis and planning to bring Tylenol back, Burke formed a seven-member strategy committee, which he chaired.* The committee met twice a day in Burke's office – early in the morning and again at the end of the day – for eight weeks. The meetings were lengthy and often marked by heated discussion and open debate, a hallmark of Burke's style of management. He not only encouraged debate on key strategy issues, he often precipitated it in order to arrive at the right decisions. Rank held no privilege in Burke's debates. When the smoke of battle cleared and he had heard all sides, he then made the final decision.

Communications within the management of Johnson & Johnson had always been good, despite its decentralized structure. That proved to be a great asset in managing the Tylenol crisis, noted David E. Collins, Chairman of McNeil and a member of the strategy committee. "It is not possible to refine poor communications at the heights of a crisis. A crisis only magnifies imperfections," he said.

Over the next several months, hundreds of people within Johnson & Johnson and McNeil changed their normal work schedules and worked day and night toward a common goal: to save the company's reputation and bring the product back to market as a way of demonstrating the company's innocence in the crime. Reflecting on the tenor of the strategy committee meetings

---

* In addition to Chairman James E. Burke, the members of the strategy committee were David R. Clare, President; David E. Collins, Chairman of McNeil; Lawrence G. Foster, Corporate Vice President of Public Relations; George S. Frazza, General Counsel; Wayne K. Nelson, Company Group Chairman; and Arthur M. Quilty, a member of the Executive Committee.

and the pressures, David Clare, company president, later told author Martin Mayer: "We watched the news together, we lived together, we thought together, and we fought together, week after week. My memory of those months is one of unending stresses – and we still had to keep running the company in its other markets."

Many of the strategy committee's discussions revolved around issues that Johnson had addressed in his Credo. Copies of the document were kept on the table in the meeting room and referred to frequently. Often the answers were there, as Burke said later: "We had to make some of the most critical decisions in the company's history," he said, "and most of what we needed by way of direction was right there in the document. Had we not made these decisions according to the Credo, we would have broken faith with our people."

KEEPING EMPLOYEES WORLDWIDE INFORMED

One of the company's traditional strengths was its close ties to its employees, which now totaled 79,000 worldwide. In the early days, the General began calling it a "Family of Companies," and now there were 160 affiliate companies in the family, with separate managements and different missions in health care but still closely tied to the parent, Johnson & Johnson. As Burke had noted, keeping faith with employees and gaining their support during the current crisis was essential. Seven years earlier, a Worldwide Video Network had been established to improve internal communications and was now being used to keep employees informed about the latest developments with Tylenol. Video monitors, converted so they could replay cassette tapes made in the United States, were in place at two hundred plant and office locations around the world. Global delivery services were used to get the tapes there quickly. Twelve hours of tapes on developments in the Tylenol story were made in the New Brunswick studio, keeping employees informed and giving them a sense of involvement.

In the final analysis, it was the public that would render the final decision on how responsible the company was and on whether Tylenol capsules would be restored to its once lofty position among pain-relief medications. To keep informed about what the public was thinking, photographers with video cameras were sent out every day, in various cities, to conduct informal, on-the-street interviews. They asked consumers their opinions about the Tylenol situation, how they thought the company was responding, and whether they would be likely to purchase the product again later. At the end of each day, the photographers would send the tape cassettes to New Brunswick by the fastest means so the strategy committee and others in management could screen them carefully. Many nights, Burke would take the tapes home and review them again, looking for guidance from the public's reaction.

The outbreak of product-tampering in the nation was now accelerating at an alarming rate, with various other companies and their customers becoming the targets of the attacks. Hydrochloric acid turned up in eye drops, and a strong irritant was found in a bottle of mouthwash. Shoppers had become wary and were now examining packaging for signs of tampering. When they became suspicious, they complained to store clerks. A tension had been added to shopping. In Washington, the FDA and Congress were working feverishly to come up with emergency legislation that would soon revolutionize consumer packaging with regulations on tamper-resistant packaging. There was no way to fully protect consumers from product contamination, but the new requirements for tamper-resistant packaging would at least provide some safeguards. It was clear that what began as one company's problem had now become society's problem.

As the relaunch of Tylenol capsules moved forward, consumer surveys were encouraging. Some 79 percent of those polled now said they would buy Tylenol again, in tamper-resistant packaging. "We are sensing a tremendous reservoir of goodwill and trust toward Johnson & Johnson and the brand," Burke told the *Wall Street Journal* with a note of optimism.

THE COMEBACK MARKETING STRATEGY

The marketing strategy for the relaunch was rapidly taking shape, and the new packaging equipment had been purchased and was being installed on production lines faster than anyone had thought possible, because people were working day and night. Several years earlier, the public-relations agency Burson-Marsteller had been retained by McNeil to publicize the Tylenol brand. The agency suggested that the capsules be reintroduced at a televised press conference that would be beamed via satellite to press conferences held simultaneously across the nation in dozens of other cities, thereby ensuring wider coverage by the news media. Management bought the idea, and the elaborate planning began.

In early November not even six weeks after the crisis began, the new Tylenol packaging was introduced to the McNeil sales force. The bottles included three tamper-resistant seals: an outer box with all the flaps glued shut, a red plastic band sealing the cap to the neck of the bottle, and a strong innerfoil seal over the mouth of the bottle. The design of the triple safety-sealed packaging went beyond the new requirements being drawn up in Washington, which would take effect in a few months. A race developed within the drug industry to see who would be on the market first. McNeil President Joseph R. Chiesa announced that the cost of the new packaging – two cents a bottle – would not be passed along to consumers but would be absorbed by the company.

The marketing effort moved into high gear, drawing on all the company's strengths. A huge task force of 2,250 sales people recruited from domestic Johnson & Johnson companies that marketed professional products was briefed on the Tylenol relaunch. They were assigned to help the McNeil sales force make presentations to physicians and other health-care professionals, with the target being one million visits. Thirty McNeil sales managers were given television training, and after the introduction they made appearances on more than one hundred local talk shows to promote Tylenol capsules in the new safety packaging.

The carefully planned relaunch took place on November 11 at the Sheraton Center in New York, where a hundred news media people had gathered for a closed-circuit television press conference that was also relayed by satellite to thirty other cities. In those locations another five hundred news people had gathered, making the turn-out one of the largest press conferences ever held. The number was high because personal invitations had been sent to every reporter who had worked on the Tylenol story. Their names and addresses were drawn from the log that the public relations staff had been keeping since the first press call.

At the press conference, the new tamper-resistant package was unveiled with great fanfare. The other news was that consumes would receive a free bottle of Tylenol capsules in the new tamper-resistant package. This clever marketing scheme would be backed by a massive advertising campaign, aptly named "Thank you, America," and include distribution of 80 million coupons worth $2.50 each when redeemed for the capsules. The rest would be up to the public, Burke said. "We are confident that consumers will make an eminently fair decision about the future of Tylenol, " he told the press, which relayed the message in thousands of news stories about the comeback.

The public responded favorably, and sales of Tylenol capsules began to soar. In less than a year, the product had regained its preeminent position among pain-relief medications. Johnson & Johnson's reputation was intact, and the news media gave the company high marks for its performance during the crisis. The *Washington Post* said: "Johnson & Johnson has effectively demonstrated how a major business ought to handle a disaster." At Johnson & Johnson, much of the credit was being given to Robert Wood Johnson's philosophy of managing a business.

THE HORROR OF 1982 IS REPEATED

Three years and three months later, the unthinkable happened. On February 8, 1986, a young woman from Westchester County, New York, died of cyanide poisoning after ingesting a Tylenol capsule. Other capsules in the bottle had also been contaminated with potassium cyanide, but in this case the chemical profile was slightly different from the cyanide used in the Chicago murders. Tylenol capsules were promptly removed from store shelves in the immediate area. It was February 10 before the medical tests were completed and the press was on the story. The search for the killer focused on Westchester County because the improbability that the poisoning occurred during manufacturing had been established in 1982. The story was once again on the front pages, reviving all the horrors of the unsolved mystery in Chicago. Old television footage showed bottles of Tylenol being swept off store shelves in Illinois. The nightmare had begun again for the people at Johnson & Johnson and McNeil. They were devastated.

On Tuesday, February 11, the company called a press conference at corporate headquarters in New Brunswick for that afternoon. There was a wicked snowstorm that day. At the company's request, AT&T and New Jersey Bell worked feverishly to set up telephone lines to enable the news media from all over the nation to listen in on the news conference. Seventy members of the press came to New Brunswick. Seven hundred other news media people were on the telephone hookup. There was little news to offer, but the company wanted to show that it was cooperating with the press, as it had in 1982. No immediate recall was planned, Burke told the reporters. There were questions about the tamper-resistant packaging and how it had apparently failed. The contaminated bottle sold in Westchester had been manufactured in Fort Washington eight months earlier.

On Thursday there was a baffling development. A second bottle of contaminated Tylenol capsules was found on a store shelf in Westchester County. The bottle had never been opened – its safety seals were still in place. But the contaminated, discolored capsules could be seen through the bottom of the bottle, which had been produced in Puerto Rico seven months earlier. Investigators examined the bottle and found no visible signs of tampering, but it was sent to the FBI labs in Washington for closer testing.

Johnson & Johnson held another press conference in New Brunswick, where questions were asked about how the bottle could have been invaded and contaminated with the safety seals still in place. No one had an answer for that. Burke made it clear that Johnson & Johnson was itself a victim, again, and that the company was reluctant to give in to a terrorist. The investigation in Westchester had made no progress, but authorities believed there was no link between the crime there and the murders in Chicago three years before.

STRATEGY COMMITTEE TURNS TO THE CREDO

In desperation, fourteen states banned the sale of Tylenol capsules. All across the nation there were reports of suspicious deaths and attempts to link them with Tylenol. Even where the evidence was sparse, overzealous reporters made it a big story, and the national frenzy was regenerated. A report came from Washington that the FBI had discovered how the terrorist had invaded the bottle taken from the store shelf in Westchester, but the technique was wisely withheld. The news was reassuring to the company, though no one believed the contamination could have taken place at the plant. It was a terrorist act, and in the three years since the Chicago murders the feeling that it could happen again had not diminished.

The strategy committee, reconvened by Burke, met later the same day to resolve a crucial question: Should Tylenol capsules be removed from the market? There was no easy answer. Sales of the product had soared to $550 million a year, with profits exceeding $90 million, making it a major contributor to the company's overall financial performance. Then there was the important consideration of employee morale. Hundreds of people had worked tirelessly over a long period to restore the product to its leading position in the analgesic market – and many had said it couldn't be done. Would it be fair to them to summarily wipe out their hard-earned achievement by abandoning Tylenol capsules? Those at the meeting who had worked hardest on the comeback stoutly defended keeping the product on the market and resolving the present difficulties, just as had been done before.

In time, the discussion turned to the Credo. Everyone in the room knew that it would. A copy of the Credo lay on the table around which the group was seated. Its presence there was disquieting. Someone raised a difficult question: If a terrorist had demonstrated that it was possible to invade the safety-sealed bottle without it being detected, how could customers ever be protected from danger? No one had the answer. Then came another question: If the first responsibility under the Credo was to the customer, wasn't there only one decision to be made? Burke set up a press conference for the next morning.

JOHNSON & JOHNSON DOES THE RIGHT THING

Standing before the crowd of news media representatives the following day, Burke announced that Johnson & Johnson would discontinue manufacturing all over-the-counter capsule products worldwide. "We feel that the company can no longer guarantee the safety of capsules," he said. Then he held up a large model of a Tylenol Caplet – a white, oval tablet that was virtually tamper proof. The company, he said, would replace all the capsules now in the hands of retailers and consumers with the new caplets. As he spoke, cameras pressed closer for a photo of Burke holding the model caplet with the red Tylenol logo emblazoned on the side. He paused, and for a minute only the sound of clicking cameras could be heard. The next day, the photo of Burke holding the enlarged caplet ran on front pages all across the nation, including the *New York Times*.

It appeared to be a carefully orchestrated marketing presentation, but it wasn't. Hours earlier, when the strategy committee concluded that the Credo had spoken, they pondered:

What now? They turned their attention to Tylenol Caplets. McNeil had developed the caplet product in the aftermath of the 1982 crisis, and it had modest success. As luck would have it, however, a huge quantity of caplets had just recently been produced for a special sales promotion and were sitting in a warehouse waiting to be distributed. The caplet model that Burke held up at the press conference was actually an old paperweight given away as a promotion at the time caplets were introduced. A secretary in public relations remembered seeing one on a desk in the building and borrowed it for the photo. It was perfect.

Four days later, at the National Press Club in Washington, President Ronald Reagan was addressing a group of business leaders and the press. He departed from his prepared remarks to praise Burke and Johnson & Johnson for the actions that had been taken in the public interest. As it turned out, consumers all over the nation shared these sentiments, and Tylenol Caplets became an overnight success.

Somewhere, Robert Wood Johnson must have been smiling. His Credo had helped to write the end of the story.

THE CREDO LIVES ON IN THE FAMILY OF COMPANIES

In the decade since becoming Chairman and CEO of Johnson & Johnson in 1989, Ralph S. Larsen skillfully blended the Credo principles into the mainstream of several management programs aimed at strengthening the company. As a result, he brought a new dimension of importance and utilitarian value to the Credo, lifting it beyond its traditional role of being a statement of responsible decision-making and making it a management tool. The process that the Credo has gone through in making these further contributions to the company's success is a tribute both to Robert Wood Johnson's foresight and to advancements that have been made in the art of management.

The 1982 Tylenol crisis thrust the Credo into the limelight, and the news media began referring to the document as the most widely known statement on corporate responsibility in American business. The passage of time did nothing to detract from the document's visibility. Some sixteen years later, in his 1998 book, *Eighty Exemplary Ethics Statements*, Professor Patrick E. Murphy, Chair of the Department of Marketing at the University of Notre Dame, wrote: "The Johnson & Johnson Credo is probably the best known ethics statement in the world, at least partially due to the central role it played in the tragic Tylenol poisonings."

The higher the pedestal, the more likely it is to be shaken when something goes wrong. The rocking of the pedestal came in 1983 when Zomax, McNeil's popular new prescription drug for intense pain, was linked to more than a dozen deaths caused by the severe allergic reaction known as anaphylaxis, which can lead to seizures and respiratory failure. While nearly 15 million patients were using Zomax without untoward incident, the recurrence of anaphylactic reaction sounded an alarm and prompted critics to ask: "Where was the Johnson & Johnson Credo in this scenario?"

McNeil's response was that the risks of taking Zomax – an oral drug as effective as injected morphine, but one that did not cloud the consciousness or cause addiction – were stressed in instructions to physicians. Unfortunately, the warnings were not always heeded. Despite the merits of the drug, Johnson & Johnson decided to voluntarily withdraw the product from the market when reports of anaphylactic reactions continued. The Food and Drug Administration was not happy with that decision because of the unique need Zomax filled for patients with intractable pain. The drug's supporters said the company had acted precipitously, but its critics said action was not swift enough. The merits of both arguments were debated in ensuing litigation.

BEGINNING OF THE CREDO SURVEY

This watershed event moved the Credo to a new level of importance within Johnson & Johnson and its Family of Companies. In the Tylenol episode, the company had been seen as a victim. With Zomax, the circumstances were different, and while the Credo had precipitated the decision to withdraw the product from the market, there was the question of timing. It was now abundantly clear that all future decisions of major importance made by the company would be measured against the yardstick that the Credo had become. Previously, Johnson & Johnson had been judging itself by these standards. Now the outside world was doing so as well. The Credo's new visibility brought added responsibility and made the company more vulnerable to criticism.

Sensing the Credo's new importance, Chief Executive Officer James E. Burke and his colleagues launched in 1985 a new program to make the document as relevant to employees as it had become to management. Known as the Credo Survey Process, it would become the foundation on which the next Chairman, Ralph S. Larsen, and his management would build.

The process began with a carefully thought-out questionnaire that would allow the company's employees to evaluate how management was performing in the four areas of responsibility covered in the Credo: consumers, employees, communities, and the stockholders. To encourage frankness, employees were assured that all responses would be held confidential. A special staff was assigned to handle the survey and the evaluation. After a test run at one of the affiliate companies, the Credo Survey Process was expanded to cover all of Johnson & Johnson's 77,000 employees worldwide. The complex survey took months to complete.

Asking employees what they thought of management's performance in carrying out the goals of the Credo was not without risk – but it was deemed a risk worth taking. The responses were tabulated and analyzed, and the results were given to managers, who then held feedback meetings with their people. At these sessions, deficiencies in the workplace and in other areas where the company was not performing to employee expectations were discussed. Managers were then required to present action plans to correct problems the survey had revealed.

MAKING JOHNSON & JOHNSON A BETTER COMPANY

At the end of the lengthy process, even skeptical employees seemed to have a new respect for what the Credo could accomplish in making Johnson & Johnson a better company.

Cultural differences, and the way overseas managers viewed the American concept of corporate responsibility, made the Credo more difficult to comprehend, and follow, for certain Johnson & Johnson international affiliates. Senior managers devoted a great deal of time to this learning process.

When a Japanese business delegation interested in promoting their nation's economic development came to the United States, one of their stops was to visit Johnson & Johnson's corporate headquarters in New Brunswick, New Jersey. Surprisingly, they focused on the Credo and came armed with penetrating questions about its effectiveness. While meeting with four members of the company's Executive Committee, they asked: "Can you give us an example of an important decision that was rescinded because it was in conflict with your Credo values?"

This was the reply: "One of our affiliate companies had recommended we close a textile operation because it was no longer profitable. In doing so the company would have been forced to close a plant in the South in an area already hard-hit economically. Many of our long-service employees, some with twenty to twenty-five years, would have been put out of work. When this decision came to the Executive Committee, the discussion centered on our Credo responsibilities. As a result, the plan was substantially altered. We asked one of our companies looking to expand to move into the plant to be vacated. They did, and we were able to utilize some two hundred people that otherwise would have been displaced. We also altered the severance and relocation programs for the remaining employees. Basically, this was about our Credo responsibilities."

RALPH LARSEN REINFORCES THE CREDO

When Ralph Larsen became Chairman, he began finding new ways to use the Credo as a management tool. An executive in Human Resources cited some of the objectives: "Our ultimate objective," he said, "is to have employees and their managements work together to enhance our culture and strengthen the business. Increasingly, employee feedback has been playing a key role in the startup of task forces and action plans aimed at improving the workplace. The survey process is no longer just a report card. It serves as an instrument with enormous potential to increase employee involvement, productivity, and the communication of values and business objectives. It is also a means of getting employee input into forming strategic plans."

The Credo Survey Process was now put on a bi-annual schedule and demonstrating that it was capable of identifying and resolving gaps between its guiding principles and the company's daily action. The Credo's reputation in business was growing. In 1991, *Business Ethics* magazine cited it as a legendary document "and perhaps the nation's longest lasting and most effective statement of corporate ethical standards."

Expanding rapidly, Johnson & Johnson now had more than 150 affiliate companies around the world, and this complicated the task of applying the Credo principles to such a wide range of cultures and business practices. In preparation for the Worldwide Management Conference in 1995, an "Executive Survey of Credo Values" was sent to 246 senior managers. They responded with a list of significant components they felt would be required if Chairman Larsen were to achieve his goal of creating what he described as a "Credo-based leadership."

The managers decided that Credo leadership would require daily management behavior that supported the values outlined in the document, that communications about Credo values had to be purposeful and consistent, and that the company's reward system had to include recognition of management adherence to Credo principles. By wisely allowing manages to set the ground rules, Larsen was ensuring support for the program. From this, one of the conference's major themes evolved and was titled "What Does It Mean to Be a Credo Leader . . . *Specifically.*"

INTRODUCING "STANDARDS OF LEADERSHIP"

At this major conference of company management, Larsen made it clear that Credo leadership *at all levels* was needed to sustain the integrity of Credo values in a highly competitive global marketplace. The next step in the evolution of the Credo was a major new program titled "Standards of Leadership." In describing what was expected of management leaders, Larsen said: "Credo values represent the foundation stone upon which leadership is built. Certainly within Johnson & Johnson you cannot be a good leader if you don't believe in and try to live up to the Credo."

The "Standards of Leadership" as defined by Ralph Larsen and his colleagues embodied the following: renewed focus on the customer and the marketplace, innovation, interdependent partnering, organizational and people development, and mastering complexity. These goals, they said, defined the fundamental requirements for maintaining leadership in the global marketplace. To serve this purpose, the "Standards" became the driving force behind a series of human resources programs, and the focal point of discussion and review of the Succession Planning Process. In short, that determined who moved up in the organization and who didn't.

Of all his business skills, Robert Wood Johnson's talent for selecting and training a highly competent management paid the biggest dividends. For decades the company had been widely recognized for developing outstanding management – *Forbes* magazine referred to Johnson & Johnson as "one of the world's best managed companies." As with other successes in business, the last best performance becomes the launching pad for higher achievement if the upward momentum is to continue.

ATTAINING A COMPETITIVE ADVANTAGE

Chairman Larsen saw a problem on the horizon. Early in 1998, he wrote his senior management around the world: "It is increasingly evident that the competitive nature of the marketplace goes far beyond the issues of market share, product technology, and shareholder return. We are seeing increased competition for talent as well. A shortage of management talent can be a key restraint in achieving growth and performance objectives. Competition for top talent will become increasingly fierce. . . . It will be only your continued emphasis on leadership development that will enable Johnson & Johnson to retain our talented people for future growth opportunities."

In the highly competitive global game of attracting and keeping talented management, Johnson & Johnson's trump card has been the Credo. The principles expressed in the document are appealing to the type of person the company wants to attract. Some other companies subscribe to similarly high standards of conduct, but few are as overtly committed to a written set of guidelines as Johnson & Johnson.

At the important succession planning meetings, when upward mobility in the company is discussed with managers, "Credo Values" is first on the agenda. "Business Results" is next in line. The behaviors associated with Credo values are noted: "Behaving with honesty and integrity. Treating others with dignity and respect. Applying Credo values. Using Credo survey results to improve the business. Balancing the interests of all constituents. Managing for the long term."

Like his predecessors, Ralph Larsen had to deal with violations of Credo policy and did so swiftly, clearly outlining the consequences of such infractions. One incident involved infiltration of a competitor's sales meeting. Larsen wrote his management: "Our behavior should deeply embarrass everyone associated with Johnson & Johnson. Our investigation revealed that certain employees had engaged in improper activities that violated our policies. These actions were wrong and we took steps, immediately, to discipline those involved and guard against a recurrence of this kind of activity."

It is better for global managements to assimilate the philosophy contained in the Credo than to have it force-fed to them. All six Johnson & Johnson Chief Executive Officers, beginning with Johnson, and then Hofmann, Sellars, Burke, Larsen and now Bill Weldon, have been acutely aware of that. Managers have never been ordered to display the Credo, but they do with remarkable frequency. When professor and author Patrick Murphy visited the Janseen-Cilag pharmaceutical affiliate in Cork, Ireland, he noted: "An enlarged Credo hung both in the reception area and outside the managing director's office." Had he been in Malaysia, he would have seen what is referred to as the "Credo Wall" – the document translated into twenty-four languages.

J&J COMPANIES WORLDWIDE TRANSLATE THE CREDO

To make a point regarding the universality of the Credo within the company, Chairman Larsen in 1997 collected sixty-five copies of the Credo in various languages and had them printed in a single volume. In his foreword to that book, he wrote: "We share a heritage so strong that it transcends cultural and language differences. The bond that ties us all together is Our Credo, a simple yet profound document that clearly defines our responsibilities. . . . As you will see in the following pages, Our Credo looks different from country to country. But no matter what the language, its enduring principles remind us of the values that make up the character of Johnson & Johnson."

There has always been a pocket of criticism in business that dismisses such high-sounding philosophy as merely a form of self-delusion – that business success is more about numbers than it is about integrity and putting the customer first. Johnson & Johnson's reply, of course, is that its "numbers" have been consistently good throughout the company's history.

BILL WELDON CARRIES ON CREDO LEADERSHIP

William C. Weldon succeeded Ralph Larsen as Chairman and CEO, and immediately stressed the importance of the Credo as being the very fabric of Johnson & Johnson's enduring culture.

"It guides our decision making and it is the basis for what I believe is our most competitive advantage – that is our value system," he told a meeting of company management. "If I can embody the tenets of the Credo then I can live proudly as just one in a long line of leaders – leaders like everyone represented here who will be the people who create the future for Johnson & Johnson."

Expressing further thoughts on the relevance of the Credo in today's complex world, Chairman Weldon recently said:

"For more than 60 years, Our Credo has been the compass that has guided us through significant change across the Johnson & Johnson Family of Companies as well as within our industry. Today, it continues to be the bedrock upon which we honor our responsibilities to our customers, employees, communities, and stakeholders around the world.

"Inspired by the work of dedicated men and women, we are touching over a billion people a day with our products and services. Our Credo is a reminder of the special purpose we serve and the broad responsibilities we have in meeting the healthcare needs of patients and customers.

"Throughout Johnson & Johnson we rely on the voices of our employees in helping us shape a work ethic and environment that allows us to achieve excellence in our important mission of serving patients and customers."

GLOBAL LEADERSHIP PROFILE ANCHORED BY CREDO

In 1995, Bill Weldon was part of a team of senior leaders who formalized the first leadership framework, known as the Standards of Leadership. Since the inception there have been two upgrades. In 2000, an assessment by leaders around the world made recommended changes to enhance the global nature of the leadership framework and to place a greater emphasis on the Credo as the foundation of the program. The program evolved to "The Global Leadership Profile" and the Credo more than ever sets the standards of behavior expected of the Leaders.

The Executive Committee has been directly tied to the Company's expectations and goals as they relate to Credo Values Training. The Executive Committee Leadership and Growth Meeting is conducted annually and attended by the top 120 managers. There is in-depth skills development for all new managers. Credo Values Dialogues center around Johnson & Johnson case studies which require leaders to work their way through addressing ethical dilemmas that arise when managing the world's largest and most diversified health care company.

COMPANY GROUP CHAIRMEN DIRECTLY INVOLVED

Now that the company's franchises are a focal point of the Survey process, Company Group Chairmen are in a position to examine the way in which their managers are carrying out their Credo responsibilities. And then their responsibility is to take action where indicated.

What began as a far-sighted declaration of the responsibility a corporation has to serve the public interest – the Credo written by Robert Wood Johnson in 1943 – has evolved into a sophisticated management oversight program unique to Johnson & Johnson. No other company in the world can match the way this responsibility and conduct is monitored.

Bill Weldon sees adherence to the Credo as his most important responsibility, as have the Johnson & Johnson chairmen before him. This is what makes Johnson & Johnson and its Family of Companies such a special place to work.

THE CREDO IN ACADEMIA

Robert Wood Johnson's Credo has become the best known statement of corporate responsibility in the business world. Because of its relevance to good business practice, and the need to expand on the lessons it teaches, it was made part of the Arthur W. Page Center for Integrity in Public Communication at Penn State University's College of Communications in 2004.

This affiliation with the nation's largest accredited college of communications provides students and academic researchers from all over the country, and internationally as well, the opportunity to explore ways that the Credo's challenges can have greater influence on business decisions and communications to the public. A similar challenge is presented by the Page Principles, guidelines reflecting the teachings of Arthur W. Page, a legendary figure who was the nation's first person in a public relations position to serve as a corporate officer (AT&T from 1927 to 1946). Page was also a distinguished statesman and educator.

The affiliation of Robert Wood Johnson with Penn State was made possible by major gifts from The Robert Wood Johnson Foundation, Betty Johnson and Woody Johnson for The Robert Wood Johnson 1962 Charitable Trust, and four of Johnson's colleagues, James E. Burke, David R. Clare, Richard B. Sellars and Lawrence G. Foster.

The Page Center is under the direction of Dr. John S. Nichols, Associate Dean, Graduate Studies and Research. He can be reached at jsn2@psu.edu.

ABOUT THE AUTHOR

Larry Foster was night editor of the Newark News in New Jersey before joining Johnson & Johnson in 1957 to help form its first public relations department. He was Director of Public Relations and Assistant to the Chairman before becoming Corporate Vice President of Public Relations. During his 33 years with Johnson & Johnson he reported to three Chairmen/CEOs.

He was managing public relations at Johnson & Johnson when the company was widely acclaimed for its handling of the Tylenol crises in 1982 and 1986. His professional awards include the Alexander Hamilton Medal (2007) from the Institute for Public Relations, the Gold Anvil (1989) and the Atlas Award (1998) from the Public Relations Society of America, and the Hall of Fame Award (1994) from the Arthur W. Page Society. He was president of the Arthur W. Page Society (1990-92), and chairman of The Wisemen (1986-90). PRWeek named him one of the ten most influential public relations professionals of the 20th century.

He is author of three books: A Company That Cares, a history of Johnson & Johnson (1986); the biography, Robert Wood Johnson: The Gentleman Rebel (1999); and Robert Wood Johnson and His Credo: A Living Legacy (2008).

For 16 years he was a trustee of the Robert Wood Johnson Foundation in Princeton, N.J., the nation's largest health care philanthropy.

He is a founder and chairman of the Advisory Board of the Arthur W. Page Center for Integrity in Public Communication at Penn State University's College of Communications.

A 1948 graduate of Penn State, he received the Distinguished Alumnus Award and the Lion's Paw Medal for service to the University. He was a University Trustee and president of the Alumni Association. He and his wife, Ellen Miller Foster, Penn State Class of 1949, live in State College, Pa., and Westfield, N.J. They have five children and ten grandchildren.

"Reading this book gave new meaning to my job."

"I gave a copy of this fascinating book to everyone in my group."

"Elegantly written . . . Anecdotally fascinating."
John Cunniff, The Associated Press

* Comments about *Robert Wood Johnson: The Gentleman Rebel*

ROBERT WOOD JOHNSON
AND HIS CREDO
A Living Legacy

A Condensation of
Robert Wood Johnson: The Gentleman Rebel

(published in 2008)

$7.00 plus shipping

TO ORDER

US and Canada	Fax	From Overseas
800-247-6553	419-281-6883	419-281-1802

Or online at *www.atlasbooks.com*

ROBERT WOOD JOHNSON
THE GENTLEMAN REBEL
The Biography of Robert Wood Johnson

(published in 1999)

$30 plus shipping
$250 for a case of 10 books